quiet reflections of peace

120 Devotions to End Your Day

quiet reflections
of peace

Revell
a division of Baker Publishing Group
Grand Rapids, Michigan

© 2009 by The Livingstone Corporation

Published by Revell
a division of Baker Publishing Group
P.O. Box 6287, Grand Rapids, MI 49516-6287
www.revellbooks.com

Printed in China

ISBN 0-978-0-8007-1929-6

Produced with the assistance of The Livingstone Corporation (www.
LivingstoneCorp.com). Project staff include Betsy Schmitt, Linda Taylor, Linda
Washington, Dana Niesluchowski. Cover and interior designs by Larry Taylor
and Lindsay Galvin. Production by Larry Taylor and Lindsay Galvin.

Welcome

What's the perfect way to end your day? Receiving a hug and a toothpaste-scented kiss from your child? Brewing a cup of decaf tea and putting your feet up? Being able to read your favorite novel quietly without constant interruption? A warm bubble bath? The perfect way to end a day is to spend time with God—to tell Him how you spent your day and to relax in His presence as day turns to dusk. God offers encouragement and strength through His Word as you surrender your fears or frustrations.

To facilitate your time with God, we offer 120 meditations for the evening. Each meditation includes a Scripture passage, an inspirational thought, an ending prayer, and a beautiful color photo based on the themes discussed. Consider the prayer a jumping-off point to your own conversation with God.

You're invited to follow in the footsteps of Nicodemus, who came to Jesus at night with his questions (John 3:2) and received insights he had never even considered! As you prepare to sink into sleep, take a few moments with your Savior. He wants to give you quiet reflections of peace to end your day.

—*The Editors*

Contributors

Judith Costello
Elizabeth C. Hubbard
Pat Stockett Johnston
Kathy Lay
Diane Markins
Heather M. Pleier
Alene Snodgrass
Ann Swindell
Linda Washington

He took Abram outside and said, "Now look up at the sky and count the stars, if you are able to count them." He also said to him, "That's how many descendants you will have!"

Genesis 15:5

As Numerous as Stars

Stretched out on a blanket in the cool crisp grass late in the summer evening, you gaze into the night sky. In the country, away from the glare of city or suburbia, the stars stand out, vivid and bright. As stars blend into galaxies upon galaxies, it is impossible to count them.

Imagine Abram staring into that same night sky thousands of years ago. He, too, had a wish. For a child, a descendant to carry on the family name and tradition. Yet, when God promised him that he and Sarai would have as many descendants as the stars in the night sky, well, that was too much to hope for. They were too old. Their time was running out. Impossible, they thought.

Has God spoken something into the still of your soul and you are just wishing it will come to pass? Or like Abram and Sarai, you think time has run out for you. You can't imagine how such a thing will ever come true for you. You are left wishing for a shooting star.

Tonight, put your faith in God alone and rest. The writer of Hebrews reminds you, "Faith assures us of things we expect and convinces us of the existence of things we cannot see" (Hebrews 11:1).

As you gaze into the beauty and mystery of the night sky, raise your hopes and dreams to God. Wait on Him to bestow blessings on you as numerous as the stars in the sky.

Lord,

help me rest this evening
as I give You my hopes
and dreams. Forgive me
when I doubt You, O Lord,
increase my faith. Thank
You for the vastness of
Your universe. Remind me
that Your blessings are as
numerous as the stars.

Lord God,

I lay my worries at Your feet. Thank You, Lord, for the mighty ways You deliver me. You are my rock and shield.

The LORD is my rock and my fortress and my Savior, my God, my rock in whom I take refuge, my shield, the strength of my salvation, my stronghold, my refuge, and my Savior who saved me from violence. The LORD should be praised.
2 Samuel 22:2–4

One Smooth Stone

Five smooth stones were used. But only one was needed. For forty days, Goliath, a nine-foot-tall Philistine giant, mocked the Israelites and their God. Brave warriors were terrified of what Goliath could do.

Young David arrived on the scene and was instantly outraged by Goliath's remarks. While his brother tried to discourage him from getting involved, David was stirred by his confidence in God. With five smooth stones and his sling in hand, David set out to conquer his enemy in the name of the Lord God Almighty. Knowing that the Lord would deliver him from his enemy, David triumphed with just one small stone.

Years later, after facing many enemies, David used the rock image in a psalm describing his confidence in God. God was his rock—the only one needed to defeat any enemy (Psalm 18). God delivered David from all of his enemies and made him king over Israel. Therefore, David could rest the full weight of his trust in God.

What enemies are taunting you tonight? Maybe your giant is your health, finances, addictions, a hectic schedule, or rebellious children. Such enemies taunt us and rob us of sleep. When trouble beckons, call on the Lord God Almighty. As your rock, fortress, and shield, He is a source of strength. Run to Him for shelter.

The battle is the Lord's. With faith in God, you will triumph.

> *God didn't give us a cowardly spirit but a spirit of power,*
> *love, and good judgment.*
> 2 Timothy 1:7

Fearless

ear. According to psychologists, it is one of the most powerful emotions we can experience. It can cause us to take drastic
action or paralyze us into inaction. It can make us lose sleep, lose
weight, and lose reason. In short; it can control us.

Life seems to be filled with perils—real or only anticipated. A
conflict with your husband. A scheduled meeting with your child's
principal. An overdue bill in the mail. We often fear what we don't
know or even what we think might happen.

Are you plagued by fear tonight about what will happen tomorrow? As you lay in the cold grip of fear, remember that spirit of fear
didn't come from God. So where did it come from? We have a powerful enemy who whispers into our thoughts and fuels emotions of
dread, worry, helplessness, and fear.

Take back control! As the apostle Paul explained to his spiritual
son, Timothy, God has given you a spirit of "power, love and good
judgment." That means you can handle any situation with His help. Be
confident in His promise and cover yourself in a blanket of God's love
as soon as your head touches the pillow tonight. Rest in God's ability
to conquer the spirit of fear.

A Father,

I don't like the way fear feels. Help me have courage and confidence in Your ability instead of giving in to fear.

Father,

help me to look to You, to remember how You have been faithful. Remind me of the ways You have worked in my life.

Lovingly, you will lead the people you have saved.
Powerfully, you will guide them to your holy dwelling.
Exodus 15:13

Looking Back for Hope

After leaving a life of slavery in Egypt, the people of Israel traveled to the Red Sea, only to be trapped by the sea with the Egyptian army in pursuit. Their situation had now moved from hopeful to hopeless.

Or so it seemed.

In the midst of their helplessness, God provided a path through the Red Sea. He then caused the Egyptian army to drown in the sea—thus saving the people of Israel (see Exodus 14).

Moses and the people celebrated the victory by singing the song from which today's verse is derived. They knew God would continue to provide for His people, just as He always provided. He would lead them to the Promised Land. They had only to remember their past to find comfort in their present.

Think back to the times that you have seen God move powerfully in your life. How did He work in ways that seemed impossible at the time? Sadly, we sometimes take for granted the things He has done. Or, we think we have to fight the battles on our own and forget that our loving Father can and will provide for His children.

Tonight, in the midst of life and all its uncertainties, consider God's promise of guidance. He will never start you on a journey only to abandon you in the middle of it. Tonight, let the words of assurance spoken by Moses guide you to a place of rest.

When you lie down, you will not be afraid. As you lie there,
your sleep will be sweet.
Proverbs 3:24

Sweet Sleep

*Y*ou know the days when you wake up refreshed after a good night's rest. You feel as if you can conquer the world! But there are some nights where you feel overwhelmed by what tomorrow may bring. With the day's worries running through your mind, it is impossible to close your eyes and rest. Sweet sleep eludes you.

The anxiety that comes as a result of a busy, chaotic world is nothing new. As you read through the Bible, you learn about many people who were also burdened by anxieties, distractions, and fear. Perhaps that's why wise King Solomon included the above promise in his wisdom advice. He knew that peace was one of the promises God gave to Israel during their time in the wilderness (see Leviticus 26:6). If your heart is at war, peaceful sleep is difficult to gain.

That's why Solomon highlighted the value of clinging to the wisdom of God. As we trust God, our "sleep will be sweet."

God knows you need sound slumber to feel refreshed. Meditate on the verse above. Remember that God provides you with a quiet place of rest for a sweet sleep that refreshes.

Heavenly Father,

take away the frantic worries in
my mind. Slow down my thoughts
and cause me rest in You. As I lay
here tonight, give me sweet sleep.
Refresh my soul as I sleep.

Heavenly Father

hear my cry for help. Give
my heart an extra amount
of strength tonight so
that I may begin climbing
again tomorrow.

Listen to my cry for help, O God. Pay attention to my prayer.
From the ends of the earth, I call to you when I begin to lose
heart. Lead me to the Rock that is high above me.
Psalm 61:1–2

A Tough Climb

Sometimes at night, small problems can loom like giant mountains. Even goals we set, which were not meant to be problems, can seem overwhelming. The challenge then turns into a frustration that causes you to lose heart.

Consider the discipline it takes to climb a mountain. Even if you've never climbed one, you can appreciate the struggle up that rocky face and the triumph of reaching the top. Many times during the journey, a climber might be tempted to give up.

Reaching a goal can seem like climbing a mountain. David, the shepherd turned king, was no stranger to the challenges of life. After all, he spent over a decade on the run from King Saul who wanted him dead. After being anointed king and finally ascending the throne, David's goal was to unite all of Israel. But David knew that the challenge of ruling a divided people could be surmounted by God, "the Rock that is high above." God was his place of refuge and strength.

If your commitment is waning, cry out to God just as David did. From the ends of the earth He will hear your prayer. He knows that your goal is a tough climb and offers His help. Each step you take together brings you one step closer to conquering your goal.

When you're frustrated and feeling overwhelmed by the challenges along the way, turn to God, your Rock, to help you. From the ends of the earth, He will answer.

He will not let you fall. Your guardian will not fall asleep.
Indeed, the Guardian of Israel never rests or sleeps.
Psalm 121:3–4

Sleep Tight, Little One

If you have children, you've probably spent many nights watching over as they slept—especially when they were babies. Perhaps you have little ones right now. You watch their every exhale and inhale, and make sure they are comfortable. You can't take your eyes off their small frames as they lie there nestled in bed. Perhaps you pray they will have sweet dreams and feel secure as they sleep. Quietly you whisper, "Sleep tight, little one. Sleep tight."

Don't you long for someone to have that kind of watchful care over you? The security that you provide your little ones is only a fraction of what your heavenly Father provides for you. As the psalmist explains, the Lord is "your guardian." Because He never sleeps, He can offer protection throughout the night. He will never take His eyes off of you.

Restful sleep comes with knowing that you're cared for. Problems during the day have a tendency to crowd our minds. We find ourselves counting sheep and worries. That's why it's great to know that a big God watches over you. He can handle those worries while you sleep. His watchful love says to you, "Sleep tight."

Lay your head down, close your eyes, and know that the Maker of the Universe, Creator of the Heavens and the Guardian of Israel is up tonight watching over you. "The eyes of the LORD are everywhere" (Proverbs 15:3).

Heavenly Father,

thank You for the ways
You watch over me. Thank
You for the assurance that
You will always keep me
secure. I'm glad You never
tire or forget to watch over
me. Because of Your love,
I can sleep tight.

✿ *Father,*

today was hard, and I need to rest. Help me remember that You are big enough to handle my problems, no matter how serious they are, and big enough to provide for my family's needs. When I can't sleep, give me words of comfort and hope. I love You, Father.

When I lie down, I ask, "When will I get up?" But the evening is long, and I'm exhausted from tossing about until dawn.

Job 7:4

Finding Rest

Job had every reason to complain. His children had died, his wealth was gone, and his body was covered with painful boils (Job 1–2). He was miserable during the day, and the nights seemed unbearably long as he tossed and turned, unable to find relief.

Job was ready to give up. Although he was a righteous man with faith in God, sleeplessness brought him to a breaking point; he had lost hope. But God—his Hope—never lost track of Job. Even though he allowed the pain in Job's life, God still loved Job and later gave him rest from all of his pain and anxieties.

Sleepless nights—whether from illness, children, anxiety, or any other source—can cause us to lose perspective and to forget our Hope. We find ourselves feeling hopeless in the wee hours.

Feeling a loss of hope? The Father cares about you and has promised, again and again, to give you rest. In Matthew 11:28, he calls, "Come to me, all who are tired from carrying heavy loads, and I will give you rest."

Tonight may be long and possibly sleepless. But don't give up hope. If you toss and turn, instead of being frustrated, use that time to recall songs of praise or to repeat a verse that comforts you. Remember that your Father loves you more than you could ever imagine. He has promised to comfort you through hard times and will give you rest.

*He uncovers mysteries hidden in the
darkness and brings gloom into the light.*
Job 12:22

Be Gone, Gloom

If you've ever been camping, you know the comfort of a roaring campfire. Not only is it great for roasting marshmallows and making s'mores, it also chases away the gloom of darkness. Sitting by the glowing flames, you can't help feeling safer. Noises of animals off into the distance don't sound as threatening.

In a dark place, every shadow or noise can seem threatening. That's why kids often imagine monsters coming out of closets and crave a night light. But such fears aren't just the province of children. The "monsters" in our closets aren't the cuddly ones from Monsters Inc. but real anxieties we carry to bed. Like children, we crave a light that will drive away the darkness.

Times of great testing are the dark times when we most need the light of understanding. Job faced such a time after losing all of his children, his crops, and his health. Although the time was dark and he didn't understand the reasons behind his suffering, Job knew a source of light. As he explained to his judgmental friend, Zophar, God is the light that reveals mysteries and parts the darkness. No secret is hidden from him.

Perhaps you're in a time of darkness that you don't fully understand. To release gloom and fear, turn to the Light. Best of all, this Light never needs to be plugged in!

Lord,

I need Your light to chase away my fears. Even when You don't choose to reveal every fact about a situation, I still need the light of Your presence.

Father,
cover me with a blanket
of peace and security.
Give me enough faith
to trust in You alone for
a restful night's sleep,
knowing that You are in
control of what tomorrow
brings.

I fall asleep in peace the moment I lie down because you
alone, O LORD, enable me to live securely.
Psalm 4:8

Blanketed in His Care

We all know people who can fall asleep anytime, any-place—from the dentist's chair to the back end of a roaring Harley. But most of us have to ease into slumber, letting the momentum of the day wind down and tumble off our shoulders. Can you relate?

Sometimes that restful state eludes us, not just for a few minutes as we settle in, but deep into the night. When we do fall asleep, it is fitful and strained, not bringing refreshment on the following day.

Whether we are preoccupied with our dwindling bank account, worried about the results of a blood test, or disturbed by a comment uttered by the boss, resting is not in the night's equation. But there is an antidote—a remedy for unrest. It comes in the form of a cozy blanket that covers us with safety and warms us with peace. Where do we get it? There is one exclusive source: "You alone, O LORD, enable me to live securely." Only God is able to drape us with peace and assurance in the midst of thoughts or circumstances that lead to sleepless nights. Ask Him and believe what the psalmist knew as you drift off to peaceful sleep.

I am worn out from my groaning. My eyes flood my bed every night. I soak my
couch with tears. My eyes blur from grief. . . . The LORD has heard the sound of
my crying. The LORD has heard my plea for mercy. The LORD accepts my prayer.
Psalm 6:6–9

Turning Point

When we're feeling ill and are alone, the night can loom long and seem especially miserable.

David, the psalmist, wrote about such a night, one in which he was tired, alone, and miserable due to an illness and the taunts of his enemies. With no relief in sight, he could only weep.

Many of us stop right there—at the sound of our depressed weeping. But David didn't stop. Instead, as he wrestled with his pain, he reached a turning point. Toward the end of his psalm, he wrote, "The LORD has heard my plea for mercy. The LORD accepts my prayer" (Psalm 6:9). Remembering the Lord's presence and power, he found hope and rest.

Is there something troubling you tonight? Perhaps you're facing an issue that causes the tears to spring to your eyes. Or perhaps this is one of a long series of sleepless nights where you wonder if the morning will ever come. Know that your Father is there with you. He hears you, loves you, and will answer. May you, like David, see your life reach a turning point.

Father,
I'm tired and needing rest,
but even more I need Your
peace. Hear my prayer, and
hold me close to You.

Father,

I'm grateful that You are the God of my life. I gladly trade my worries and discouragement for the night music of praise to You.

*The LORD commands his mercy during the day, and at
night his song is with me—a prayer to the God of my life.*
Psalm 42:8

A Little Night Music

In the middle of the night, what sounds do you hear? Crickets
chirping, cars rushing by, train whistles, wind rustling in the trees,
a baby's soft breathing over the monitor. They are the music of the
night—music that lulls us to sleep. These sounds are soothing,
because we expect to hear them.

Some people enjoy the quiet sound of wind chimes making their
random tunes as played by the soft night breezes. There's something about their soft, cheerful tune that makes the night seem less
gloomy. Nighttime music, to be effective, has to be soothing and
predictable. Otherwise, you can't get to sleep. So you don't expect
blaring horns, squealing guitars, discordant notes, or anything
unexpected.

One of the sons of Korah—one of the musicians King David put in
charge of worship at the tabernacle—penned a soothing psalm—
Psalm 42. Its lyrics are a litany of praise for times of discouragement.
For example: "Why are you discouraged, my soul? Why are you so
restless? Put your hope in God, because I will still praise him. He is my
savior and my God" (Psalm 42:5).

Discouragement sounds a discordant note in our lives. We feel out
of sorts and everything turns colorless. Praise has a way of dispelling
the darkness. If you find yourself tossing and turning, consider a little
night music: Psalm 42. Make it a prayer to the God of your life.

*Let go of your concerns! Then you will know that I am
God. I rule the nations. I rule the earth.*
Psalm 46:10

God's Grandeur

It's so easy to get wrapped up in the busyness of our lives.
The laundry piles up. There are the dishes, endless household
chores, work problems, and all the responsibilities of being a modern
woman. The list seems to go on and on! We find ourselves trying to
hold it all together in our minds.

But we are called to let go, and be still, as this day comes to an
end. When we set aside the "to do" lists and seek quiet—then our
hearts, eyes, and minds will be free. Silence and emptiness opens up
"mind space" in order to give God some room.

All we need to do is look beyond ourselves toward the stars
above. Then we will recognize how small our lives truly are. How
puny are those concerns that seemed so big only moments ago!
They are dwarfed by the vastness of the galaxy created by God.

Consider also the openness of the vast plains and desert lands.
Areas like the Grand Canyon or the Badlands are nothing to the vastness of the Creator—the One who rules the earth.

God has placed us in an orderly universe, on a beautiful planet,
surrounded by gently waving trees, tucked in at night by a jeweled
sky.

Look up, and you will be able to let go. We don't have to rule the
world. That's God's job!

Lord,

You are the ruler of all the earth. I surrender to the stillness and bask in the beauty of this night. The heavens and the earth respond to You. And tonight as I lay back, I return to You.

Thanks

for listening, Father. Thanks for taking me seriously and wanting me to tell You how I feel, what I think, what I'm confused about. Help me to rest tonight, knowing that You have heard me and will take care of me.

I love the LORD because he hears my voice, my pleas for mercy. I will call on him as long as I live because he turns his ear toward me.
Psalm 116:1–2

A God Who Listens

The value of a listening ear is immeasurable, especially when we have a need to share. Consider the last time you really felt heard and understood. Even if a problem you related didn't automatically disappear, perhaps you felt better, knowing that you were heard.

We all long for someone who not only listens, but also understands us and truly wants to hear what we're saying. Many children seek a listening ear at the wrong time sometimes, in our opinion! They catch us when we're on the phone or trying to get to sleep. At those times, we might brush off their concerns as trivial. "Can't it wait till morning?" we say. But when the shoe is on the other foot and we're longing for a listening ear, no concern of ours seems trivial. And some nighttime concerns cannot wait until the morning. We need someone to listen—and listen good—right now.

The writer of Psalm 116 has good news: there is a listening ear that is always tuned to you. That ear belongs to God. Just as the psalmist clung to the God who hears, we, too, can be comforted, knowing that when we pray we aren't ignored nor do we have to compete for attention.

Isn't it amazing? God, the Creator of heaven and earth, listens to you: your frustrations, tiredness, or confusion. He celebrates with you your joys, triumphs, excitement, and hope. Come to Him now, knowing that He wants to hear your voice.

*Teach them to your children, and talk about them when
you're at home or away, when you lie down or get up.*
Deuteronomy 11:19

Repeat, Repeat, Repeat

If you have children, what are some of the ways you help them learn? Perhaps you sounded out each word or letter over and over as you taught your child to read or patiently demonstrated each stitch as you taught the child to sew. Repetition is one of the ways we learned to read, play the piano, swim, drive a car, and so on. Repeating an action or a word ensures that you won't forget it.

As the people of Israel prepared to occupy the Promised Land, Moses, like a good parent, wanted to impart some final words of wisdom, since he would not be with them when they crossed the River Jordan. So, he reminded them to be faithful to God and teach His ways to their children. They could do this by repeating God's laws to themselves over and over—wherever they went. If they ran into problems, rehearsing God's promises would serve as a reminder of God's presence, power, and peace.

Worry is a hazard that causes us to forget the other perspectives and options we have. That's why repeating God's promises is a preventive measure, one that works to chase away the blahs.

As you prepare to lie down tonight, think about the signs and wonders God has worked in your life. Recall too the awesome history of our faith, culminating in the Word who became man in order to save us. These images can inspire us to a renewed commitment to obedience.

Lord,

You guided our fore-
fathers with signs and
wonders. You have also
guided me, pouring out
love and mercy. As I lie
down at the end of this
day, I renew my commit-
ment to live according to
Your commands.

Father God,

whatever I am waiting for
tonight, I place it before
You, casting these cares at
Your feet. Please help me
to wait on You with hope
as I anticipate Your work
in my life and in the lives
of those I love.

*Wait with hope for the LORD. Be strong, and let your heart
be courageous. Yes, wait with hope for the LORD.*
Psalm 27:14

Waiting with Hope

We live in a fast-paced, instant-gratification culture, where waiting is seen as a bad thing. We don't like waiting at red lights or for trains to pass. But the Bible describes many instances of God patiently waiting before acting. Over 400 years passed before God freed the people of Israel from slavery in Egypt. He waited over a millennium after that before sending His Son to earth. And he's still waiting for just the right time for that Son to return to Earth to claim His people.

David, the writer of Psalm 27, majored in waiting. Many years passed between his being anointed king (1 Samuel 16:13) and his ascending to the throne (2 Samuel 5). In Psalm 27:14, he repeats the same message twice: "wait with hope for the Lord." David took his own advice during the long years of running from Saul and various enemies.

What are you waiting on tonight? A wayward child to come home? A spouse to come back to your marriage emotionally or physically? A job that will pay the bills? Waiting can be difficult. Yet we do not wait in despair. We can wait with the hope that God is restoring our lives and is working things out for our good (Romans 8:28). So before you close your eyes tonight, ask God to help you wait for Him to move in specific areas in your life. Then, fall asleep with hope in your heart, knowing that God will hear your prayer.

My salvation and my glory depend on God. God is the rock of
my strength, my refuge. Trust him at all times, you people.
Pour out your hearts in his presence. God is our refuge.
Psalm 62:7–8

Pour Out Your Heart

Every day, demands are placed on our lives. Whether it is working at our job, raising our children, cooking for our family, making it to meetings and appointments on time, or cleaning our homes, certain things must get done every day. It is easy to feel like things will fall apart if we don't do things well or accomplish our tasks perfectly. Stress grows in our hearts. When this happens, it is a good thing to remember that our salvation depends on God and not on us.

Although we have many things to do every day, God is our strength, our refuge from the stressors and demands that require our attention. He is the one that we can run to, the one that we can rely on. Because of God's love for us, He will not forsake us or ignore us.

Have you had a hard day? Do you feel as if you are failing in life? "Pour out your heart" (62:8) to God before you sleep tonight. Tell Him how you feel and ask for His refreshing perspective on your life. Your salvation depends on Him, not on yourself. No matter what you do or don't do, God is the one who is taking care of you—every day. Fall asleep knowing that you are in His hands.

God,

I am overwhelmed by the demands on my life. I choose to pour out my heart to You. I put my trust in You tonight.

Lord,

I praise You for Your goodness to me! May I never forget all that You have done for me. As I sleep tonight, I ask You to refresh my spirit so that tomorrow I may speak Your praises even more.

Praise the LORD, my soul! Praise his holy name, all that is within me.
Praise the LORD, my soul, and never forget all the good he has done.
Psalm 103:1–2

Never Forget

We remember words of praise years after they are uttered. A timely "well-done" or some other pat on the back has the power to motivate you to do your best. Sometimes praise is all that keeps us going.

While God doesn't need praise, He is worthy of it all the same. With all that is within us, we are called to praise Him.

David, the ancient king of Israel and psalm writer, was known for his wholehearted worship of God. Through Psalm 103, he encourages his readers to "never forget all the good he has done." This isn't a Pollyanna notion uttered by a man who never suffered. This was a reality David lived while suffering.

As you prepare to sleep tonight, take five minutes to focus on the good things that the Lord has done for you today. Did He help you stay calm in a frustrating situation? Did He enable your child to finish an assignment well or learn a new skill? Did He provide food for your family's table? Did He bring sunshine in the middle of a cloudy day? If we look for God's presence in our day-to-day lives, we will surely see Him! Even the flowers growing outside that bring beauty to the earth are gifts from His hand—another thing for which we can praise Him. Then fall asleep with a smile on your face, knowing that God will be just as good tomorrow as He was today!

Those who cry while they plant will joyfully sing while they harvest.
The person who goes out weeping, carrying his bag of seed, will
come home singing, carrying his bundles of grain.
Psalm 126:5–6

The Changing Seasons

Depending on where you live, a change in temperature marks a change in season. Trees change colors; certain crops are sown or harvested. Just as the seasons change, the seasons of our lives change, too. A change in circumstance or a shift in age can signal the change of a season of life.

There are difficult times in our lives when sorrow is heavy in our hearts and when joy seems to have disappeared from our days. These are seasons of tears. We lose a loved one, we fail, or we don't know how we will make it through another day. We seem to reap sorrow with every passing day.

But sorrow does not last forever. The image in this psalm is a beautiful one of hope. While the person who goes out in planting season is full of sorrow, he comes back from the fields in harvesting season "joyfully singing" as he brings in the bundles of grain. What made the difference? There's a clue in verse 3: "The Lord has done spectacular things for us. We are overjoyed." Seasons change.

If you are in a crying season, know that this season will not last forever. God understands the weariness of our hearts and walks with us through every circumstance. There will be a day, too, when you will joyfully sing again.

Holy One,

in this season of tears and sorrow, I look to You as the One who never leaves me or forsakes me. Thank You for being with me in the difficult times.

Lord, please shine Your light into the anxious recesses of my mind so I can sleep peacefully tonight. Thank You for Your watchful presence.

*Light will shine in the dark for a decent person. He is
merciful, compassionate, and fair.*
Psalm 112:4

Patrolling in the Dark

When night falls with a cloak of darkness, we sometimes
wonder what may be lurking in the shadows, especially if
we're home alone. Sometimes noises around us sound threatening
and dangerous when they're really just the rhythms of nature settling
in for the night.

The doors are locked, the dog is snoring but sleep won't come
because you are on high alert against a threat—real or imagined. But
remember, even though you may be surrounded by physical darkness, God's light of protection is shining brightly in and all around
you. His is a light of compassion and mercy; He knows your fears and
wants to illuminate the peace that is available to you for the asking.

Like a guard patrolling an important building, God keeps tabs on
you. Any enemy against you has to emerge from the blackness into
God's shimmering presence to get to you. These enemies include
worries and fears. God's security sensor flood lights are set to turn
on if an intruder crosses past them. He is your protector, so relax and
trust the Lord with all the unknowns that remain in the dark.

A gentle answer turns away rage, but a harsh word stirs up anger.
Proverbs 15:1

Take It Down a Notch

What happens when you add fuel to an already raging fire? It grows even hotter, doesn't it? Sometimes the fire rages out of control. Forests and houses go up in flames to the sadness of all.

The same is true with some of the responses we make to situations of conflict. When someone yells at you, what's your first response? To yell back? When we do that, we sometimes find our resentments magnified and our sleep troubled. Some arguments rage totally out of control and relationships are irreparably damaged.

When an angry mob of Ephraimites came to him with their grievances, Gideon, one of the Judges, took the time to soothe their resentment with a wise and humble answer (see Judges 8:1–3). He didn't allow exhaustion to spur him to answer in anger or in haste.

The writer of this proverb also knew the wisdom of giving a soft, instead of a harsh answer. Instead of notching up the speed of emotions and tempers, a gentle answer takes it down a notch and helps to keep a matter from careening out of control. It defuses tempers and prevents wars.

Is there a matter you're struggling with? Perhaps someone made you angry and you're wondering how you will respond tomorrow. Take this time to pray. Ask the Lord to give you the wisdom and humility to provide "a gentle answer." Allow Him to take those feelings down a few notches and allow you to rest.

Lord,

I long to serve You more effectively by offering gentle words to the people in my life. As this day comes to a close, I quiet my racing thoughts and listen for Your quiet voice. Guide me, Father.

5

4

3

2

1

0

x1000r/min

❧ *O Lord,*

You are the Almighty, who governs life and death, beginnings and endings, blessings and destruction. Thank You for being here with me tonight. I know Your teachings and wisdom will be my light tomorrow. Trusting in this, I am ready to sleep.

At night I remember your name, O LORD, and I follow your teachings.
Psalm 119:55

Resting with the King

What do you find your mind dwelling on at night? The events of the day—good or bad? Words said or unsaid?

Consider the words of this short verse from the longest psalm in the Bible. In it, we are reminded that God is our Lord. It's a title of respect. In referring to God this way, we remember Him as the Ruler of the universe, the Supreme Being. He is the King of Kings (Revelation 17:14; 19:16).

Each of the titles for God can give us a quick glimpse into His role in our lives. It helps us understand how to relate to Him.

God is our Source.

He is our Salvation.

He is also our Comforter and Defender in times of need.

He is Mercy and Love.

When we remember His many titles, it becomes clear that He is here, on this very night, showing His great power as well as His compassion. It's good to recognize this as we prepare for sleep. The King is also our Father and we can trust deeply in Him.

As we prepare for this night of rest, we can call out "Lord" with awe and praise for the one who made everything. Then we recall His comforting presence. How kind He is to take our troubles and concerns into His hands! And if we ask, He'll give us guidance to be the best we can be tomorrow.

Does your understanding make a bird of prey fly and spread its wings toward the south? Is it by your order that the eagle flies high and makes its nest on the heights? It perches for the night on a cliff. Its fortress is on a jagged peak.
Job 39:26–28

Look Up

When life turns sour, we find ourselves reeling, trying to make sense of it all. Sometimes we look for someone to take responsibility for what's happened.

In a tailspin due to a series of tragedies in his life—the deaths of his children, the loss of his livestock, crops, and health—Job struggled to make sense of what God allowed. What had he done to cause God to allow such tragedy? He demands, "Let the Almighty answer me. Let the prosecutor write his complaint on a scroll" (Job 31:35).

Instead of justifying Himself, God instead asked Job a series of questions, the answers to which only God knew. God wanted to make Job look outside of himself and instead look to God. Job needed a merciful and all-powerful Savior.

With which areas of life do you struggle to trust the Lord? As you prepare for bed, look at the night sky and its dazzling stars. The Lord placed each of these tiny diamonds with precision. Think about the eagles on the cliffs, settling into their nests for the night. Worries and aspirations cannot move them. In the same meticulous way that Christ hung the stars and created all the creatures of the earth, He cares for His children. His loving vision for you is so much greater than your own. Release your grip on control with this knowledge and find rest.

Dear Lord,

You are the creator and
master of this universe and
of all creation. Help me trust
You. I know You have my
best interests at heart.

Dear Lord,

thank You for watching
over and protecting me.
Draw me near to You
in moments of fear and
doubt.

Even when I am afraid, I still trust you. I praise the word of God. I trust
God. I am not afraid. What can mere flesh and blood do to me?
Psalm 56:3–4

My Comforter

When you were a child, a stuffed animal or a blanket could eliminate nearly any apprehension or hurt, couldn't it? These comfort items, however, tend to lose their impact when suffering turns from the loss of a favorite toy to a grown-up variety: ailing family members, disagreeable bosses, and financial insecurity.

During the hard times of life, some seek comfort in relationships—spouses and other family members, close friends, etc. Others seek to escape or deaden the pain through less positive means: alcohol, drugs, meaningless relationships, workaholism. Yet the problems remain. Sometimes new problems emerge as a result.

David, the psalmist and famed giant killer, knew the source of ultimate comfort—God. In Psalm 56, David praises the Lord for His faithfulness and promises in the face of adversity. Having been hounded by taunting enemies for many years, David knew the peace of trusting God as his source of security. Unlike a person, God was never too busy to listen. And He had the power to conquer any enemy.

As you end this day, consider praising the Lord for His steadfastness and dependability during difficult moments. Make a list of the things that worry you. After each item, use the words of David and say to yourself, "I trust God." He alone is your comfort.

Turn all your anxiety over to God because he cares for you.
1 Peter 5:7

Two Choices

Wash your face, moisturize, brush and floss, set the alarm, turn all your anxiety over to God. It's just part of the bedtime routine. No problem, right?

Not so fast. It is much easier said than done. Is it any wonder that the subject of worry crops up time and time again in the Bible? The apostle Peter, who was with Jesus for three years, knew what his Master had to say about worry (see Matthew 6:25–34). Jesus made the point that worry doesn't add a single hour to your life and, in fact, shows lack of trust in God's promise to care for you. So Peter suggested that you take your anxiety and turn it over to God.

But how do you do that? Giving your worries to God is saying to Him, "I refuse to carry this worry because I know You already have the answer for me. I'm going to patiently wait for you to show it to me."

What is your day like when you're carrying worry? And how do you feel when you turn off the light? Dried up, exhausted. When you turn that anxiety over to God, however, you're able to flourish, to function, to move forward.

There will always be something to worry about. As you travel the road of life, you have two choices. Which side of the road do you want to be on—the side of anxiety and worry and deadness? or the side of life and health?

The answer is easy.

Dear God,

thank You for loving me.
Help me to give all of my
worries of this day to
You, trusting in Your
love for me.

Lord,

open my eyes and let me
see the love and strength
You've sent to surround
me. Show me that I'm not
fighting alone.

Elisha answered, "Don't be afraid. We have more forces on our side than they have on theirs." . . . The LORD opened the servant's eyes and let him see. The mountain around Elisha was full of fiery horses and chariots.

2 Kings 6:16–17

You're Surrounded

We love stories of bullies being defeated by the deserving underdog. But in real life the stronger one—the one holding all the power—wins, right? The bank manager who says no to your request for a loan, that unreasonable boss who makes your life or your spouse's life miserable, those who make our streets unsafe—they seem to have the power. Troubles of the day seem to have you surrounded as you try to sleep.

The Arameans—enemies of Israel—held the power in the time of Elisha. After warning the king of Israel about the plans of the Arameans, the king of Aram sent an army to capture Elisha. While his servant panicked, Elisha prayed the prayer above. The enemy may have had them surrounded. But God's army—one much more powerful—had them surrounded too.

Today, consider what surrounds you. Perhaps you're facing a wall of fears. Or, having contemplated a stack of unpaid bills, unfinished projects, or unfriendly relationships in your life, you feel totally alone, totally overwhelmed. But you are not in this alone. Whether you are fighting to get all your work done, battling a serious illness, or other threats to your peace, He is with you. His heavenly army and His powerful love surround you like a warm embrace.

As you slip under the covers, bask in the knowledge that a far more powerful ally fights for you.

Rather, he delights in the teachings of the LORD
and reflects on his teachings day and night.
Psalm 1:2

Soak It In

If there is a tree outside your bedroom window, take a minute to gaze at it. Consider its height and width.

A tree gains water and nourishment from the soil. The xylem of a tree—the cells that form the rings of a tree—enable the tree to take water out of the soil and therefore "feed" the leaves. A tree has to continually take in water to refresh its leaves. If the tree didn't take in water, the leaves would wither.

The same is true for us. While we understand the need for proper hydration, sometimes we forget to "hydrate" through the Word. Busy schedules, problems, and other obstacles keep our spiritual xylems from soaking in refreshment. Instead, we're bombarded by images and words that don't help us to grow.

In describing how a godly person "is like a tree planted beside streams—a tree that produces fruit in season and whose leaves do not wither" (Psalm 1:3), the writer of Psalm 1 described the strategy of this person: "he delights in the teachings of the LORD and reflects on his teachings day and night."

Tonight He speaks peace into your soul. He delights to fill you with His love and wisdom from His Word. After reading, close your eyes and reflect on God's truths, goodness, and faithfulness. Then take a second look at the tree outside the window. You are like that tree— fed by God's Word, growing tall in God's grace.

Heavenly Father, sometimes I'm easily distracted with responsibilities and exhausted from a busy schedule. Forgive me for the times when I forget to soak in Your Word. Thank You for Your Word and the nourishment I can find there.

 Lord,

as David said, relieve my
troubled heart. As I lift
my eyes to You, O Lord,
let me see the silver
linings and blessings You
have in store for me.

Turn to me, and have pity on me. I am lonely and oppressed.
Relieve my troubled heart, and bring me out of my distress.
Psalm 25:16–17

A Silver Lining

ome days are easier to get through than others. Perhaps
today you were reminded of how alone you feel with no
one with which to share your struggles. It's like a dark cloud hanging over you. Even with a loving family, you can still feel alone as
you contemplate problems or issues demanding a response from
you. Such feelings are often magnified at night as the darkness
closes in. You want to run, but there seems nowhere to go. You
want to scream, but there is no one to hear. You want to pray, but
wonder if God is listening.

David, the psalmist, could relate. His psalms contain some of
the most gut-wrenching cries for help that you'll find in the Bible.
This one is no exception. Though surrounded by the dark clouds of
loneliness and oppression, David didn't hold back his pain. Instead,
he grasped for the silver lining in the cloud by unabashedly calling
out for God to rescue him.

You've heard the old saying, "Every cloud has a silver lining."
Perhaps you see only the darkness of the cloud at this moment. Yet
there is a silver lining on the horizon.

God is there. Cry out to Him tonight. Share the full weight of
your discouragement or pain with Him. Ask Him to not only help
you rest tonight, but rest in the knowledge that He is looking out
for you.

When I said, "My feet are slipping," your mercy, O LORD, continued to hold me up. When I worried about many things, your assuring words soothed my soul.
Psalm 94:18–19

My Feet Are Slipping

Gymnastics is a precision sport combining tumbling and acrobatic feats. Is there anything more exciting than seeing a gymnast not only walk across but do a series of handsprings or a handstand on a narrow balance beam?

Life can sometimes seem like a balancing act—one no less compelling than that of a gymnast. On some days, you might feel extremely competent at balancing work and family schedules, household tasks, and other demands. But on other days, perhaps you feel as if your feet keep slipping on that balance beam as more demands pile up than you feel capable of meeting.

Perhaps tonight you're wondering how you can please everyone or get everything done. Or perhaps you're mourning the fact that you fell off the beam, as it were, and pleased no one—including yourself.

The writer of Psalm 94 has the perfect response for anxious times like this: call out for help. His words show the kind of SOS call that always gets God's attention.

Like the psalmist, although you may feel your feet are slipping, God will hold you up. His assuring words will soothe, and His mighty hand can sustain you through the acrobatic ventures you may face tomorrow.

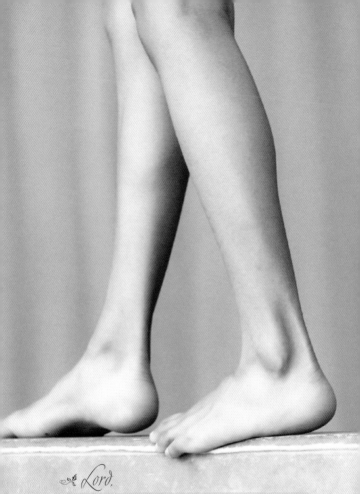

Lord,

I sense my feet are slipping. I'm weary, tired, and unfocused.
When I lose balance, please hold me up. Soothe my soul this
evening as You speak Your assuring words over me.

Holy Spirit,

in the absence of fire,
clouds, and burning
bushes, I sometimes
struggle to see You. Please
make Your presence
known to me tonight.

> By day the LORD went ahead of them in a column of smoke to lead
> them on their way. By night he went ahead of them in a column of
> fire to give them light so that they could travel by day or by night.
> Exodus 13:21

Guiding Light

If you've ever driven on a dark, foggy night, you know the
welcome relief of seeing red taillights ahead of you along the road.
There's a certain level of comfort in knowing that you're not alone in
the fog, that someone else is driving carefully along and you can stay
close and follow.

Some situations in life are just as murky. Unresolved issues in relationships, tasks for which no clear direction is given, or multiple opportunities before you can cause confusion and stress. At those times,
we need clear guidance by which to navigate and avoid trouble.

When the people of Israel left Egypt, they probably weren't sure
how they were going to get from Point A to Point B—the Promised
Land. So the Lord went before them "in a column of smoke" during
the day and "a column of fire" at night. These were visible symbols of
His presence and His commitment to guide them to the Promised
Land. Best of all, God never led them faster than their ability to travel.

In need of guidance? As the passage above shows, God is more
than capable of providing it in many forms. He may send a friend
with timely advice or provide just the right Scripture to illuminate
your situation. He also provides the warmth of His presence through
the special smile or hug of a spouse. Like those welcome red taillights, God is guiding and you can safely follow. You can rest assured
tonight knowing that the Guiding Light goes before you.

> *I lie down and sleep. I wake up again because the LORD
> continues to support me.*
> Psalm 3:5

A Protective Shield

The day is over. Or is it? Perhaps you take to bed unmet expectations, frustrations, and fears of the day. Worries wash over you like waves pounding against a shore. You feel alone and unsupported as you consider what has been done or needs to be done.

At the time King David wrote this psalm, he was running from his son Absalom, who rebelled against him and tried to take over his throne. Imagine the stress of having a family member turn against you. (Perhaps you don't have to imagine this.) Yet David was confident in the Lord's protection while he slept. As he explained in another part of the psalm, "But you, O LORD, are a shield that surrounds me. You are my glory. You hold my head high" (3:3).

God is the same for us—a protective shield from harm and fear, stronger than any enemy we face. We can sleep without fear or worry knowing that He supports us.

Every day that we wake up again is because of the Lord's continual protection and presence in our lives. As you climb into bed tonight, reflect on the ways God supported you throughout the day. Then, fall asleep knowing that He will continue to protect you.

Lord,

thank You for Your support in the night. I choose to sleep in peace this evening because I trust that You are guarding my life. May I wake tomorrow praising You for Your goodness toward me.

God,

I am thankful that Your Holy
Spirit dwells in me and that I am
Your temple. I am grateful that
Your eyes are always on me and
that You hear my prayers.

Night and day may your eyes be on this temple, the place
about which you said, "My name will be there." Listen to
me as I pray toward this place.
1 *Kings* 8:29

The Temple of the Lord

You may have had conversations where you're certain that the person you're talking to isn't really listening. Sometimes we think of prayer in the same way. Even as we pour out our hearts, we wonder if God is listening to us, or if we are only praying to the ceiling. Ever think that?

After the completion of Israel's first temple, King Solomon prayed during the dedication. Knowing that God's presence would fill the temple, Solomon asked God to listen to his prayers and trusted that God would not ignore him.

What thoughts are on your mind tonight? What hopes or concerns are in your heart? If you believe in Jesus, you are filled with His Holy Spirit and have become the new temple of God. You are treasured by the Father who loves you. As the apostle Peter explained, "The Lord's eyes are on those who do what he approves. His ears hear their prayer" (1 Peter 3:12).

As you prepare for sleep, remember that God's eyes are on you and His ears are open to your prayer. You are not praying to the ceiling. So tell Him what's on your mind this night—He is ready and willing to listen.

So Jacob was left alone. Then a man wrestled with him until dawn.
Genesis 32:24

Wrestling in the Night

So often, we wrestle with God about what is happening in our lives. And nighttime is usually when that wrestling happens. In the dark, fears and questions easily rise to the surface of our hearts.

As Jacob traveled back to his homeland to meet Esau, many fears probably rose to his heart. After all, he stole his brother Esau's birthright and deceived their father. He was not certain what type of homecoming he could expect. But just before he met Esau, he encountered a strange man who "wrestled with him until dawn" (verse 24). Neither would let the other go, and even after the man dislocated his hip, Jacob refused to stop fighting until he received a blessing.

Jacob realized that he was not wrestling against a mere man but against God (verse 30). And God was gracious to him. He received not only a blessing, but a new name: Israel, which means "He Struggles With God" (verse 28).

It is okay to "wrestle" with God—to ask Him difficult questions and cry out to Him for help and mercy. Because of Christ's death and resurrection, you are loved by God and can go "confidently to the throne of God's kindness to receive mercy and find kindness, which will help us at the right time" (Hebrews 4:16). He is the God who blesses His people. Tonight, whatever you are wrestling with God about, ask Him for His blessing, and for a new start.

God,

I have many questions and struggles, and I don't understand all that You are doing. But I come to You tonight confidently, approaching Your throne in prayer because of Jesus. I also ask for You to bless me, God—not because of who I am, but because of Your kindness and mercy.

Father,

I thank You that while I might leave things undone at the end of the day, You are faithfully and continually working in my life to make me Your beautiful masterpiece.

*I'm convinced that God, who began this good work in you, will
carry it through to completion on the day of Christ Jesus.*
Philippians 1:6

You'll Be Complete

Sometimes we go to bed at night frustrated at the tasks on our "to do" lists that are now on our "not done" lists. Many times we create lists for ourselves that are impossible to finish, or the interruptions of other activities took up the time we thought we'd have to check off the tasks on our lists.

What a relief to know that the Lord never leaves anything undone. He finishes the job at hand. That includes the work He has begun in you. When you decided to become a follower of Christ, God began changing your heart and your life. Just like any other important project, a great deal of effort and thought are being devoted to "finishing" you. Like a craftsman who carves away at a block of wood, He patiently works a piece at a time—carving here, finely sanding there.

God is a Master Craftsman, working on your life. He alone sees the finished product—and so every chip, every cut, every fine bit of sanding is creating an object of perfection.

You many not have completed everything you set out to do today, but rest assured that your list will be there tomorrow. Tonight, thank the Master Craftsman for His continued patient work with you. Remember that quality workmanship takes time and intricate crafting. You will one day be a completed work of exquisite design because God always finishes what He starts.

*Nothing can ever separate us from God's love
which Christ Jesus our Lord shows us.*
Romans 8:38

Nothing Can Separate

When we've blown it, we can't help rehashing the incident over and over in our minds. We fervently wish that we had for a "do-over"—a way to undo what was done.

Perhaps today you made some choices or said something that you feel will keep you from God. The fact that it's too late to unsay or undo what was done robs you of sleep. If so, the apostle Paul has good news: nothing in creation can separate you from the love God has for you.

As humans, our love is often based on certain conditions being met. When they aren't, our love grows cold. But God's love is unconditional—no strings are attached. It is the most powerful force in history. By the power of His love, mountains have moved, seas have parted and very old women have given birth to healthy babies. That's the kind of love that flows over you tonight. Because of His love, there is nothing that divides us and God. His love bridges any gap.

God loves you not because of your behavior, choices, or talents but because of who you are in Him. Rest your weary head on His shoulder and let His love fill your heart tonight. Nothing can keep you apart from Him.

Father,

I sometimes feel Your love is out of reach. Give me a reminder of Your precious love that is mine alone.

Father,

too often I lose sight of
eternity. I get caught up
in the details of life. Help
me to remember that
my home is in heaven.
Thank You for giving me
something to hope for.

*As Scripture says: "No eye has seen, no ear has heard,
and no mind has imagined the things that God
has prepared for those who love him."*
1 Corinthians 2:9

Mind-Boggling Goodness

What would be the most amazing thing that could happen to you in your life? Winning the lottery? Getting a 200 percent raise increase at work just because? Your husband telling you to take a week's vacation at a spa by yourself—he'll take care of the kids? Mister Perfect showing up at your doorstep tomorrow with arms full of long-stemmed red roses and a marriage proposal? A well-known TV program calling to say that your home has been selected for a million-dollar makeover? Your favorite sports team winning the national championship two years in a row?

Sometimes it's nice to dream big about our lives on earth. But we can also dream big about eternity. Perhaps you've wondered what heaven will be like. We've heard of pearly gates, streets of gold, no more crying, our own mansions, no more fear, pain, or death. Yet even with that description the Bible promises that heaven will blow our minds. Not even the wisest, the most educated, not even the greatest theologian has even an inkling of what God has prepared for those who love Him.

Tonight, as you pray, you ask God to renew your sense of wonder in the things He's promised to do for you. Pray for a sense of expectation, to not get so caught up in the mundane details of life that you forget that there's something mind-bogglingly better waiting for you. Thank Him for giving you the chance to dream.

Just as the heavens are higher than the earth, so my ways are higher than your ways, and my thoughts are higher than your thoughts.
Isaiah 55:9

Puzzling Over His Plans

We like being on the same page with someone—having a common understanding. But have you ever been in a conversation with someone and found yourself puzzling over something that was said? Many conflicts begin with a misunderstanding and continue with resentment or lack of trust.

We sometimes misunderstand God because we're uncertain of His ways. We think we have God figured out even when we sometimes lack a crucial piece of the puzzle: His input. Therefore we might limit what He could do or assume that He would do exactly what we might do in a circumstance.

In a prophecy for the exiles who would someday return to Palestine after years of captivity, God spoke through the prophet Isaiah concerning His inscrutable ways. Instead of writing off His rebellious people, God promised to show them mercy. All they had to do was return to Him. When they did, He promised to totally forget their wrong (Psalm 103:12; Isaiah 43:25).

If you're feeling yourself at an emotional distance from God due to regret or guilt, consider returning to Him. God holds all of the pieces to the puzzle. He turns mishaps and misfortunes into kingdom builders. Relax in the knowledge that He is up to something spectacular in your life!

Your heavens are beautiful. I am thankful to know Your thoughts are not my thoughts. Please make something beautiful out of my life. I don't understand, but help me trust.

Heavenly Father,

I know You care for the sparrows, but I don't feel very cared for tonight. Thank You for looking after me during this season of my life and showing me I am worth more than a sparrow.

Aren't two sparrows sold for a penny? Not one of them will fall to the ground without your Father's permission. Every hair on your head has been counted. Don't be afraid! You are worth more than many sparrows.

Matthew 10:29–31

More than Sparrows

Even if we have the veneer of "having it all together," we can sometimes feel worthless. Illnesses that rob us of strength or cause hair loss; problems in families; financial reversals—these can all eat away at our confidence and leave us wondering what tomorrow will bring.

Through the words of Jesus as recorded in the Gospel of Matthew, God reminds you that you are worth more than many sparrows. There are many different types of sparrows: House, American tree, Eurasian tree, Savannah, Black-throated, White-throated—the list continues. They are small and seemingly insignificant to some and are a nuisance to others. In Jesus' time, two could be sold for very little. However, the God of the universe always knows if they falter, fly, or fall. If He tends to the needs of these small brown birds, you can rest tonight knowing He will notice every detail of your life.

Take your fears to the Lord every moment of the day. He knows every inch of your body, having formed you in your mother's womb (Psalm 139:13–14). Just as He knows the number of hairs on your head, He knows your struggles and joys. God doesn't want you to be fearful, but trusting. Hear Him whisper tonight, "Don't be afraid! You are worth more than many sparrows."

At the same time the Spirit also helps us in our weakness, because we don't know how to pray for what we need. But the Spirit intercedes along with our groans that cannot be expressed in words.
Romans 8:26

An Amazing Language

No one understands why dolphins protect humans, but stories of them rescuing humans go back to ancient Greece. Many of the cited cases portray a person swimming in the ocean in harm's way of a shark when dolphins come to the rescue. It leaves you wondering how they communicate the need to help this victim.

Dolphins have an amazing language all their own. It's made up of squeaks, whistles, and clicks. Although we cannot hear nor understand them, they understand each other. Their communication patterns have helped save many humans from danger.

Today, perhaps you've felt as if predators lurked all around. Tonight, you cry out in your weakness not knowing what to say. You know you need to pray, but words won't come. You want to communicate your needs, but you're left speechless. There are no words—just sighs, moans, and whimpers.

Just as the dolphins communicate in a language you cannot understand, so does the Spirit of God. He hears your moans and takes them before the throne of God. Our garbled communication becomes intelligible in His capable hands.

Tonight, know that your moans are heard. Know your groans are turned into words through the Spirit. He intercedes for you, even when you don't know what to pray. It's an amazing language. He's an amazing God.

❧ Father God,

thank You for the gift of
Your Spirit. Thank You for
the way you look after
me. Thank You that You
know what to pray and
have words to express
them when I no longer
have words. You have an
amazing language for
which I have no words.

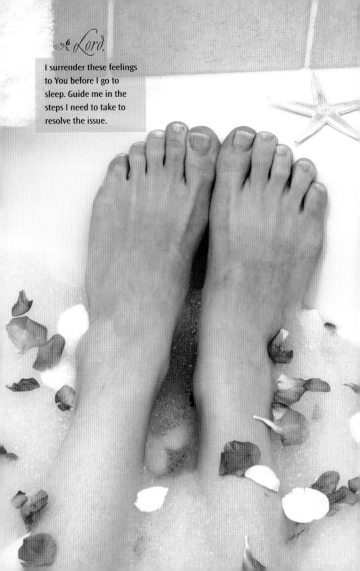

Lord,

I surrender these feelings to You before I go to sleep. Guide me in the steps I need to take to resolve the issue.

Be angry without sinning. Don't go to bed angry.
Ephesians 4:26

Take Me Away

Tonight, perhaps you find yourself quoting the famous bubble-bath advertising slogan, "Calgon, take me away!" But what sparked the need? Opposition from a family member? Tension because of an unresolved issue? Wouldn't it be great if climbing into a luxurious hot bubble bath with candles surrounding the tub permanently took away the problems of the day? We'd be there all day if that were true!

Hanging on to the incident will only cause the anger to grow to a level where it affects everything you do. It is so easy to hang on to your anger, frustrations, and wrongs. But soon you realize it is those you love the most who suffer if you are unwilling to surrender.

Want to really escape? Follow the advice of the apostle Paul. Do whatever it takes to resolve the issue. He follows up the advice above with a good reason for resolution: "Don't give the devil any opportunity to work" (Ephesians 4:27). Not wanting to give the evil one any traction, you make a conscious decision to forget, to forgive, and to make the wrong right.

By following Paul's advice, you can feel God's pure delight pouring over you as your soul unwinds. A heavenly "Calgon" moment of surrender helps take away the anger and soothe the soul.

*Always be joyful. Never stop praying. Whatever happens, give
thanks, because it is God's will in Christ Jesus that you do this.*
1 Thessalonians 5:16–18

Smile!

When was the last time someone told you to "put a smile
on your face"? Following that piece of advice is the last thing
you want to do when you're in pain. Yet perhaps you know people
who take this advice to heart out of a conviction that faking an
emotion is better than showing the world how they really feel. Is that
something you believe?

The apostle Paul was not advocating faking an emotion as he
wrote to the believers of Thessalonica. Instead, he advised his readers
to "always be joyful." While such a sentiment sounds impossible in
the face of some of life's tragedies, consider the fact that being joyful
doesn't mean hiding behind a plastered smile on your face. It means
that you know where your hope and joy ultimately lie—with the
Lord. Only the Holy Spirit can help you to "always be joyful" or to "give
thanks" even when life is at its most difficult.

The more you realize your blessings, the more you understand
how to be joyful always. As you snuggle up in bed tonight, make a
mental list of some of these blessings. Perhaps this litany of blessings
will help put a smile on your face as you drift off to sleep.

Heavenly Father,

help me be joyful always. You have blessed me in many ways. No matter the circumstances, my hope is in You.

Heavenly Father,

open my mind to Your
truths and wisdom.
Forgive me when I search
for answers in the wrong
places. Tonight, as I read
Your Word, provide the
wisdom I need.

If any of you needs wisdom to know what you should do, you should ask God, and he will give it to you. God is generous to everyone and doesn't find fault with them. When you ask for something, don't have any doubts.

James 1:5–6

Just Ask

Who do you turn to for advice? A friend or family member? Your pastor? Or do you turn to the advice offered by celebrities, magazines, and the Internet? Some searches for advice depend on the level of desperation or the level of resources available. If you're desperate, you might turn to the first available source you can find or to those you can afford. But sometimes these sources of wisdom aren't very wise at all.

Perhaps you're searching for answers right now but aren't sure where to turn for wise guidance—especially in the middle of the night. If so, James the brother of Jesus has some advice for you: turn to God tonight for the wisdom and the knowledge you seek. Generously, He gives answers to those who seek His counsel. His answers and awesome solutions come from His Word or through the wise counsel of others who seek Him. Best of all, you don't have to pay a fortune to attain it.

Tonight, ask God for a supply of His never-ending wisdom. As you drift off in the still of the night, answers will assuredly come.

Remember the LORD of Armies is holy. He is the One you
should fear and the one you should be terrified of.
Isaiah 8:13

In the Midst of the Storm

The fear of the unknown is often worse than the imagined event. It can keep you awake at night fretting about the right decision or outcome. It can also make you feel as if you're about to face a horrible storm without any protection or provisions.

Knowing of His people's tendency to fear the unknown, God spoke a warning to the prophet Isaiah. God's prophet was not to fear the anger or disapproval of the people as he preached God's promise of the destruction of the northern kingdom of Israel and the Arameans at the hands of the Assyrians. While the people of Judah might delight at the destruction of their enemies, Isaiah could not rejoice, for he knew that the event was an act of judgment on God's part because of His people's great disobedience. God reminded Isaiah and the people of Judah that the Lord was the only One they were to fear.

Tonight, perhaps you feel as if the storm is upon you. Whether it is your marriage, your relationship with others, or ethical decisions to be made at work, remember Isaiah's words. The Lord of the Armies is the One to fear. But this kind of fear is healthy fear; it's the kind of fear that understands God's great power and rests in awe of it. Remember, He is with you. In the midst of the storm, His sun will shine for you.

Heavenly Father,

watch over me. As I sleep
tonight, please bring
peace and wisdom in the
midst of the storm of my
life. Thank You for being
the Lord of the Armies.

Father,

You are in control, and
You are capable. Help
me to fall asleep tonight
putting all my worries in
Your capable hands and
trusting You to provide.

> *"You put everything under his control." When God put*
> *everything under his Son's control, nothing was left out.*
> Hebrews 2:8

Large and in Charge

What would a typical day be like if everything seemed totally in control? Would your kids be perfectly behaved with no screaming fits, no lost homework, no complaints about food, no arguments about whose turn it is to do the dishes? Would they go to bed exactly when they're told without an argument? Would your co-workers and supervisor praise you and cooperate? Seems like a fantasy. After all, life is messy, life is hard, and it very often feels like we've lost control. We feel like a person in a runaway hot-air balloon, struggling with the ballast to maintain control.

Perhaps you've had an out-of-control day that has left you feeling exhausted tonight. How great it is, though, that we have a God who doesn't lose control. In fact, the writer of Hebrews specially mentions that "nothing was left out" of God's control. Even all the tiny details of our day that we so often forget, He has under His control.

Tonight, rest easy in the arms of the God who has absolutely everything under control. Trust Him to provide for you as He has promised. No matter how much comes your way, it will never be too much, because your heavenly Father is in charge, and He knows what He's doing. He's the only one who is really large and in charge.

*I, the LORD, watch over it. I water it continually. I watch
over it day and night so that no one will harm it.*
Isaiah 27:3

Well-Tended

To be watched over, fed, and protected by the Most High, the All-Powerful God—what a picture of tenderness and strength, affection, and care. It is akin to a huge NFL football star rushing home every night to check on his African violets, hurrying down to the kitchen every morning to check for any new blooms, to trim off any old, and to carefully check the soil for moisture and health.

The prophet Isaiah preached a message of the future deliverance of Israel. In it he described God's people as a vineyard carefully nurtured by God. A good vineyard owner kept his or her vineyard watered and protected. Watering a vineyard "continually" in the arid climate of Palestine took a tremendous amount of effort. So the image Isaiah provides shows the efforts God promised to make on behalf of His people. His nurturing would cause His people to thrive.

As God's people—the church—we can take this message to heart as well. Often, we're so caught up in helping others to thrive that we neglect our own growth. But God promises to carefully watch over His little tender "plants." He waters you through His Word and protects you.

Let the wonder of God's concern sink in tonight as you get ready for bed. Know that even as you sleep, your heavenly Father is here, guiding your path and protecting you. His unfailing love for you is evident today, tonight, and tomorrow.

❧ *Father,*

thank You for always
paying attention to the
details of my life, and for
promising to protect me.
You are powerful, and
You will provide.

Father,

these decisions are not
easy. I need Your help
to know which path to
choose, which decision is
the right one. Show me
Your way, and give me the
strength to walk it.

This is what the LORD says: Stand at the crossroads and look. Ask which paths are the old, reliable paths. Ask which way leads to blessings. Live that way, and find a resting place for yourselves.
Jeremiah 6:16

At the Crossroads

Standing at the crossroads—what image does that bring to mind? Detective movies where the skilled sleuth confronts two possible roads on which the kidnapper's car traveled? Robert Frost's poem, "The Road Not Taken," which begins, "Two roads diverged in a yellow wood"? Or, perhaps you think of an unmarked, country intersection when you've taken a detour or shortcut and are trying to find your way back to the main highway.

In trying to convince a wayward people to return to Him, God spoke the message above through the prophet Jeremiah. He reminded them to consider how their ancestors worshiped God. This was the road to follow. The other road, the road of rebellion that led to their present predicament (threatened with invasion), had led them astray. So, they had a choice to make.

We're often faced with difficult choices. Knowing that these choices are not always straightforward, our heavenly Father has given us some guidelines in making these tough, life-changing decisions. We can find these "tried and true" paths in the Bible and through the wise counsel of others.

Tonight, pray for guidance and for clarity with the big decisions facing you and those you love. Pray that He will show you the right path to take and for the courage to walk that path.

He was the source of life, and that life was the light for humanity. The light shines in the dark, and the dark has never extinguished it.
John 1:4–5

The Real Eternal Flame

All over the world, eternal flames—torches that burn continually—are lit to commemorate the lives of those lost in war or to some other tragedy. This symbol of never-ending fire transcends cultures and even generations as it honors life and recognizes loss. But these flames, however well-intended and well-constructed, go out. A strong wind or rain comes along, the government regime changes, or the supply of oil doesn't get replenished, and the flame is gone.

Even the Olympic flame—carried by a series of runners over many months to ignite the torch wherever the games are held—eventually goes out.

How different, then, is the light that Jesus brought into the world, as the apostle John explains. The darkness has never and will never extinguish this light! We can have hope, because our Savior, the source of life, has come to us and lived among us.

And it keeps getting better. Through the Holy Spirit, this flame now lives inside each of us. Even when life seems hard and dark, even when that light seems dim and distant, we can trust that what God has promised is true. He has promised to guide us, to be with us, and to light our way. Tonight, as you turn off your bedside light, remember the light that burns inside of you: Jesus in you.

Father,

thank You for Your
promise of always being
with me. May the flame
of Your Holy Spirit burn
strong within me, casting
away darkness. May I take
Your light into the world.

✣Father,

what a promise! Thank
You for being willing
to guard me. Guard my
heart, guard my mind,
and guard my spirit
tonight, tomorrow, and
in the months and years
to come.

God can guard you so that you don't fall and so that you can be full
of joy as you stand in his glorious presence without fault.
Jude 24

The Ultimate Guardian

Lifeguards, security guards, border guards, guard dogs, the coast guard, crossing guards, computer safeguards, Check-Guard—there are many types of guards in our society to make sure we're doing the right thing and to prevent us from getting into trouble. Some of these guards, particularly the computer safeguards, can seem troublesome with their constant demands for safety checks and upgrades. Nevertheless, we know they are there to keep our files secure from viruses and other hazards.

Just as we have this earthly protection, the Bible promises that God also guards us. He protects us not only from the physical dangers we encounter but also guards our joy. He can keep us from being tempted to do those things we shouldn't so that in heaven we can celebrate His presence without shame. Unlike the earthly guards that go off duty sometimes, God is never off duty.

What might prevent you from asking for His protection tonight? A sense of self-sufficiency, perhaps, or a guilty pleasure that you know you shouldn't continue? Or perhaps you wonder if God really will do for you what Jude the brother of Jesus described.

Jesus calls to you to trust that He will do what He promised: to guard you until you reach His "glorious presence." Are you willing?

You will be God's children without any faults among people
who are crooked and corrupt. You will shine like stars among
them in the world as you hold firmly to the word of life.
Philippians 2:15–16

Star-Lit

What must the night sky have looked like two thousand years ago, before incandescent bulbs, jets flying overhead, searchlights advertising the new mall that just opened up across town, street lights, industrial pollution, high rises and radio towers with their airplane-warning antennae blinking on top?

It must have been brilliant and mysterious. The sun sets, and the first stars appear in the twilight, out of "nowhere," peppering the sky, until the black is awash with pinpoints of light twinkling as far as the eye can see.

This is the picture the Philippians had in mind as Paul called them to live differently from those around them. He called them, and he calls us, to consciously move away from the normal patterns of this world—and to live in such a way that we "shine." This is not easy. We want to complain when we're forced to wait for an hour at the dentist's office. Don't they know how precious our time is? We want to argue when our neighbor complains that our lawn is not up to his or her standards. But we are called to be different so that through us the light of our Father in heaven can touch the heart of our neighbor, or maybe the receptionist at the dentist office, so that she might also find the love that we have found in Jesus Christ our Lord.

Tonight, commit to shining like a star—living in such a way that God is honored.

❧ Father,

it's hard to hold back
sometimes. I want to
argue or complain. I want
people to know that I
have rights, and I want
to stick up for them. But,
just as You gave all You
had on my behalf, help
me to also show humility.

Father,

thanks for the encourage-
ment tonight. It's been a
hard day. Help me to hear
the words of support that
You give me and to sleep
well, knowing Your peace.

*A person's anxiety will weigh him down, but an
encouraging word makes him joyful.*
Proverbs 12:25

Tipping the Scales

It starts gradually—something unexpected arises, there's a change of plans, the weather doesn't cooperate, and what started out to be a good day suddenly turns into stress. Anxiety tips the scales of your life as you feel a headache coming on, the blood pressure rising, and everything turning into a big deal. You start wondering how you're ever going to make it through the day.

And then a friend calls just to say hi and that she's thinking of you. You talk for a couple of minutes, and suddenly, the scale tips once again as the world rights itself, and you remember to breathe again.

Our heavenly Father knew we needed that. He put us here, not to live alone, but to support each other. He gives us friends, brothers and sisters, and sometimes complete strangers, to remind us of those basic promises: "You're special." "You're beautiful." "You're doing a good job; keep up the hard work." "You know what, you're fantastic!" or even "Don't worry; God can handle it" when you're faced with those days that might seem overwhelming. God sends His messengers to help you remember His promises.

Tonight, thank God for the people He has given you to encourage you. Ask Him to show you who might need that same encouraging word tomorrow.

With my soul I long for you at night. Yes, with my spirit I eagerly look for you. When your guiding principles are on earth, those who live in the world learn to do what is right.

Isaiah 26:9

Eagerly Looking

During the day we're on task and productive. When the stillness of the night closes in, however, we're left with time to ponder over things we've done or said in the midst of our demanding life—things that escaped us in our busyness, but stand out boldly in the solitude of evening. "Why was I so short with my mom?" "I really overreacted to that comment at work." "How could I have forgotten to ask Sue about her doctor appointment?" It is then that we realize how much or how little we've involved the Lord in our day. It is then that our souls focus on God. In those quiet moments, we long to be closer, more attentive. We want to learn His principles so that we do more right than wrong in the course of our days. With Isaiah we cry out, "I long for you at night. Yes, with my spirit I eagerly look for you."

God's Word gives clarity and wisdom to apply to daily living. As you make your search for the Lord (and all He is) a part of your nightly ritual, as you eagerly look for Him, you will see that He is waiting for you. The more evening moments you spend eagerly looking for Him, the more your character will resemble His in the mornings.

So in these quiet moments, trust that as you eagerly search for God, He is waiting for you. He promises guidance, wisdom, and yes, forgiveness. He will give you blessed rest so that tomorrow you will be ready to walk into the new day with Him.

Father,

let me be disciplined in
seeking You each night.
Thank You for loving me
all the more as I try to
learn Your ways.

 Lord,

thank You for never shutting me out
and always having just what I need,
even when everyone else is asleep.

Your gates will always be open. They will never be closed day or
night so that people may bring you the wealth of nations.
Isaiah 60:11

Open 24/7

If you have to fill a prescription in the middle of the night, you know the value of an all-night pharmacy. Or, if you discover at midnight that you need milk for the morning, you understand the worth of a grocery store that is always open. And then there's the diner on the corner that's open in the wee hours of the morning when you're up and out early and need that first cup of coffee.

The image described in this verse from the book of Isaiah relates to a Jerusalem restored by the glory of the Lord. No longer would the city be locked up tight against invading armies. Instead, it would be open to all. Nations would bring wealth, instead of taking the wealth of Jerusalem's citizens.

What does your spirit need tonight? Whether you are longing for comfort, wisdom, courage, or a simple confirmation that you're loved, you will not be denied. The Lord is always open for business.

As you close your eyes, picture that "open" sign at your favorite all-night drugstore or coffee shop—that inviting neon that lets you know they're open for business. Then remember that access to God is also always "open." Walk through and know that He is always there for you whenever you need Him, even in the middle of the night.

*After sending the people away, he went up a mountain to
pray by himself. When evening came, he was there alone.*
Matthew 14:23

A Bit of Solitude

When bedtime finally comes and the only sound is the
night settling in, what do you do first? Do you grab the re-
mote off your nightstand and flip to a rerun of your favorite old sitcom?
Do you search for the ads in the newspaper to see who's having the
best sales on new shoes? Or do you take this time to be alone with
God?

Jesus knew what it was like to be surrounded by people demanding His attention all day. What they asked of Him was all-consuming
and He was the only one who could deliver. For those reasons, He
made it a priority to slip away from everyone in the dark of night to
spend time with His Father.

Do you have times of solitude where you can talk freely to your
Father? As day becomes night and the day's work is over, find a place
where you can hear from the Lord a little easier than through the din
of the busy day. You may find that solitude in the middle of your bed,
snuggled up in your robe on the sofa, or soaking in a warm tub. The
important thing is to find a private place to meet your Lord and pray.

Lord,

You understand how it feels to have people needing something from You all the time. Thank You for always being there to meet me in my quiet place, bringing peace in that precious time alone with You.

I desire

to wear Your wisdom, O
God, like a beautiful piece
of jewelry. As I try to
obey Your will for my life,
thank You for faithfully
giving me rest and peace.

My son, obey the command of your father, and do not disregard the teachings of your mother. . . . Hang them around your neck. When you walk around, they will lead you. When you lie down, they will watch over you.

Proverbs 6:20–22

Deal of a Lifetime

Remember going to bed when you were little? Some of us had bedtime rituals as children that included being tucked in and praying with a parent. When such a ritual becomes ingrained within us, we can't help passing it on to our children.

These verses in Proverbs encourage the passing on of knowledge. While they can be taken literally, the verses are meant to show the importance of learning to apply wisdom permanently to our lives. Imagine putting on the most beautiful necklace you can ever imagine. Putting on wisdom is like wearing a priceless piece of jewelry. Wisdom will add depth, honor, and the ability to live more confidently. When we walk in the wisdom the Lord provides, He will keep us on the right path and remove all obstacles.

The last line is especially comforting. It refers to one of the covenant blessings from Leviticus 26:6: "I will bring peace to your land. You will lie down with no one to scare you."

When we follow God, we enter into a special deal with Him. He has laid out some specific guidelines to follow and promises that when we do, He'll bless us in special ways for our obedience. No deal you'll ever be offered or contract you'll ever sign will be this easy, direct, or as completely fulfilled. It's very simple: seek and apply His teachings to your life and He will fill your sleepless nights with peace. Are you in?

My soul waits for the LORD more than those who watch for the
morning, more than those who watch for the morning.
Psalm 130:6

Waiting on Him

Some nights the ticking of the bedside clock sounds like a beating drum. We long for the Lord to make His presence known and bring with Him peaceful music to quiet the sounds of wakefulness. We glance frequently toward the window hoping His comforting spirit will win the race and beat the gray light of morning. We toss and turn, never comfortable, and even when we close our eyes we don't drift off.

The writer of Psalm 130 eloquently expressed what it means to wait in wakefulness on the Lord. Wakefulness and waiting indicate an unmet need or expectation. What are you waiting for? For the pain to subside? For God's intervention in a stressful situation? Waiting on the Lord isn't an empty exercise but an act of worship. Waiting means expecting Him to answer.

As you wait, lay your head gently on the pillow. Know that the Holy Spirit is already with you and offers more comfort than you could imagine. He is peace and promises to meet your needs. Let His presence lull you to sleep knowing that He is able to handle all your worries and problems.

Dear God,

allow me to accept the
peace You long to pour over
me in my bed right now.

Jesus,

even when I don't have
words, You know my
heart. You see my tears
and hold me tenderly
as the emotions are re-
leased, promising a fresh
perspective tomorrow.

*His anger lasts only a moment. His favor lasts a lifetime. Weeping
may last for the night, but there is a song of joy in the morning.*
Psalm 30:5

Weeping, Then Joy

Our emotions often rise closer to the surface at night. We success-
fully bury feelings of loneliness, sadness, fear, longing, or shame
as we move double-time during the day, but at bedtime they can rise
up. We sometimes put our minds through endless loops of memory
tapes— of regrets from our past or "what ifs" from the future as we lie
awake in the dark. On occasion, the swell of it is too big and must be
released. Then we weep.

God created us as emotional beings. David, the king of Israel, was
considered to be a man after God's own heart (1 Samuel 13:14; 16:12).
As one who wholeheartedly worshiped the Lord, he didn't hold back
when it came to expressing his feelings. Some of the most emotionally vivid psalms in the Bible were penned by David. No stranger to
nights of weeping, David provides a message of hope even in the
midst of a time of weeping.

Being overtaken by your out-of-control emotions is only for a little
while. Don't deny yourself the right to cry, but let your tears fall in the
lap of One who cares most: Jesus.

Remember the times God took you through an emotion-filled
night, never leaving you to weep alone. He loves you. You are one of
His favorites. This is true for all time. And, while you may be burdened
tonight, He promises to fill your heart with a different emotion
tomorrow: Joy.

*As I lie on my bed, I remember you. Through the long
hours of the night, I think about you.*
Psalm 63:6

Remember Him Tonight

Lying down at night, supported by the familiar comfort of your own bed, do you sometimes find that while your body is tired, your mind is wide awake? What occupies your thoughts? Are your emotions or worries robbing you of sound sleep? Sometimes our emotions, like the rapids of a river, continually carry us away even as we struggle back toward the shores of sleep.

David the psalmist–king probably had many sleepless nights too, but he redirected his emotion-filled soul to thoughts of God. All through Psalm 63, David describes attributes of God such as His power, His love, and His mercy. He considered the times when God came to his rescue. In short, David determined to praise rather than focus on his worries.

While you lie awake, you can take control of your thoughts just as David did and release the tight grip your emotions have on you. Let your mind focus on the One who holds all your concerns in His loving hands. Be assured that He is full of mercy, grace, and *for* you in your warm bed this minute.

Remember all that He did for David. What wouldn't He do for you? What couldn't He do? Not one of your concerns is too big or remotely impossible for the God of David, who is also your God. Ease into sleep with David's song of praise filling your soul.

 Lord,

as I lie awake tonight, I
am reminded that Your
power and love know
no limits. I will turn my
emotion-filled mind to
thoughts of praising You.

Father,

thank You for planting
in my heart the seeds of
faith. It blossoms now in
the peace that is beyond
anything I could have
imagined. You are the
Source of peace.

In every situation let God know what you need in prayers and requests while giving thanks. Then God's peace, which goes beyond anything we can imagine, will guard your thoughts and emotions through Christ Jesus.
Philippians 4:6–7

Unimaginable Peace

If you have ever spent the day gardening, you know this kind of work will give you stiff knees and an aching back. But gardening is also wonderfully rewarding. Any time spent connecting with the earth is life affirming. Best of all, when bedtime comes after a day of physical work, sleep feels absolutely delicious!

Prayer is a form of nighttime gardening. We till the soil by creating regular prayer times. Then we plant our worries in the enveloping soil of God's love. Expressing thanks for this opportunity for spiritual growth, we are blessed with an immediate harvest. A deep sense of peace settles over our bodies, allowing us to drift gently into sleep.

This passage is almost a "how to" manual for our nighttime garden. The apostle Paul tells us to begin by expressing our needs and requests in the form of prayers. We add to each prayer an expression of gratitude. Before God answers us, we offer thanks. By doing this we are saying, "I trust in You, Lord. I know You are listening and will help me." Through these simple acts of faith, we are freed from worry. Our burdens are planted in the dark of night. Peace is the harvest of a prayer garden.

Tonight is a great time to begin planting prayer and reaping peace! Ask Jesus to watch over the seeds you have planted. Then when you lie back on your pillow, sleep comes quickly.

You are my hope, O Almighty LORD. You have been my confidence ever since I was young. I depended on you before I was born. You took me from my mother's womb. My songs of praise constantly speak about you.
Psalm 71:5–6

God Was Here

Imagine for a moment the psalmist David flipping through the mental photo album of his life as he writes this psalm. He's not young anymore—perhaps he's an old man as he flips through the events of his life. "There are my father and mother and brothers before I was born. . . . There's me as a baby. . . . That's when I was watching the sheep and playing my harp—those were good days. . . . Oh, and my friend Jonathan—what a good friend he was. . . . There's me when I first was crowned king. . . ." He recognizes that in every phase of his life, even the hard times, the words "God was here" were written on each event.

In your life, it is no different. God has been just as present in every stage—even before you knew Him, even when you couldn't sense His presence. As you prepare for bed tonight, flip back through your own photo albums of memories. Think about how God has been present and faithful in each of those snapshots. You, too, could take a sticky note and plaster the words "God was here" on the photo album pages of your life. Every step of the way, right from the start, He has been by your side and will continue to be in the future.

Father,

I want to thank You
tonight for Your constant
faithfulness to me.
Thanks for guiding me
through the good times
and the not-so-easy times.
You are my hope, my
sovereign Lord.

And both his
Disciples

SNP

August, 1918

Lord,

I am grateful for Your
mercy and faithfulness. I
celebrate You as the Lord
of my life.

To the one who made the great lights—because his mercy endures forever.
The sun to rule the day—because his mercy endures forever. The moon and
stars to rule the night—because his mercy endures forever.
Psalm 136:7–9

Forever

What do you think of as you gaze at the moon and stars? While we might admire the beauty of a full moon and twinkling stars or take for granted that they are always present in the sky, the psalm writer used the moon and stars as signs of God's faithfulness and worthiness of worship. They are a testimony to the continuation of the seasons. The sun rises and sets, the moon waxes and wanes, the stars twinkle, and the years pass, all because of God's faithfulness.

Consider God's involvement in the seasons of your life. If you were to narrate your life or the events of your family as signs of His faithfulness, what events would you include? Perhaps your narration would go something like this: "To the One who healed my sister—because His mercy endures forever"; "To the One who gave my husband his job—because His mercy endures forever"; "To the One who gives us food to eat and a warm home to sleep in—because His mercy endures forever." Make this psalm your song—your chance to praise God for His presence and care for you. His mercy, His kindness, His faithfulness, and His love endure forever.

We know that all things work together for the good for those who
love God—those whom he has called according to his plan.
Romans 8:28

Planned Out

Sometimes your day is so packed with activity that it's hard to think even five minutes ahead, let alone five days. But God knows what is ahead for you. Long ago, He planned out all of the days of your life: "Every day of my life was recorded in your book before one of them had taken place" (Psalm 139:16).

Knowing that your days are already prepared by God is a comforting thought. He has a plan for your life—one that is not random or confusing, but one full of purpose and meaning. God loves you and has the best for you, and this can give you hope even when it does not seem as though everything is working out for your good. The apostle Paul penned this powerful message—one that we don't always understand during the hard times. What you are unable to understand today is something that God will somehow use for your good and for His glory. Nothing is ever lost with God; all things will indeed work together for good.

God calls you His daughter, and His plan for your life is good and important. As you lie down tonight, meditate on God's kindness and on His Word—and trust that He is working everything out in your life for good.

Father God,

I'm grateful that the plans that You have for me are good. I trust You with my life, God, because I know that You care for me.

Thank You,

God, for Your faithfulness
toward me every day of
my life. Tonight I praise
You for the ways You have
protected me even when
I have not known it. Your
faithfulness is my blanket
tonight, God. I can sleep
soundly under it.

*The Lord is faithful and will strengthen you
and protect you against the evil one.*
2 Thessalonians 3:3

Perfect Faithfulness

What do you think of when you consider the word faithful? Geysers like Old Faithful? Friends or family members who are consistently "there" for you? Encarta World English Dictionary defines faithful as "consistently trustworthy and loyal, especially to a person, a promise, or duty." Yet even the most faithful of family members or friends sometimes falter in faithfulness, depending on their own life situations. Perhaps having experienced the disloyalty of others, you wonder if it is possible to ever find someone who is faithful.

The apostle Paul makes a strong case for the faithfulness of God. He encouraged his readers to rely on God to protect them against the harmful actions of "worthless and evil people" (3:2), actions inspired by the primary enemy of Christians—the "evil one" (Satan). In a time of persecution, a time when the believers in and around Thessalonica probably felt powerless, this was undoubtedly a comforting message.

As you prepare for sleep this evening, meditate on the faithfulness of God. What events in your life have more clearly revealed His faithfulness? As you think about these things, remember that because of your relationship to God through Christ Jesus, God is on your side. He will never waver in His devotion and loyalty to you.

Pray in the Spirit in every situation. Use every kind of prayer and
request there is. For the same reason be alert. Use every kind of
effort and make every kind of request for all of God's people.
Ephesians 6:18

Ways to Pray

There are so many different ways to communicate with others. We can call or send an e-mail, a telegram, a fax, or a text message. But when the phone lines are down or your Internet service provider is experiencing technical problems, communication is difficult.

In his letter to the Ephesian believers, the apostle Paul encouraged another kind of communication: prayer. The Holy Spirit is the means for this form of communication. Since He lives within each believer, we don't have to depend on technology to communicate with Him.

Nighttime is a great time to explore different ways to express yourself to God. Tonight, try praying in a different way than you usually do. If you usually speak your prayers to God, try singing to Him. If you usually pray on your knees, pray standing up instead. God is relational, and He wants an intimate relationship with you. Talking to God is a beautiful way to grow in intimacy with Him.

As you pray to God tonight, you don't need to use fancy words or spiritual-sounding phrases. Ask the Holy Spirit to help you express your heart to God and connect with God's heart. You can also request His help and blessing for others. Enjoy communing with the Creator of the Universe, who loves you.

Holy Spirit,

please help me to pray
and to know what to
pray for. May nighttime
be a special time where I
can know You more and
express my love to You.

God,

I confess that I sometimes have a difficult time trusting You. Instead I focus on my troubles and fears. But tonight I choose to trust in You, because You alone are worthy of my trust. Please grant to me Your perfect peace as I fall asleep tonight.

> *With perfect peace you will protect those whose minds cannot be changed, because they trust you. Trust the LORD always, because the LORD, the LORD alone, is an everlasting rock.*
>
> Isaiah 26:3–4

Intentionally Stubborn

In our culture, if you refuse to change your mind about something, others may think that you are stubborn, old fashioned, or even rude. We live in a world where many people do not have strong convictions and, therefore, change their minds as easily as they change their shoes.

But there is something worth being stubborn about—trusting in God! This verse in Isaiah speaks of how those who trust in the Lord have minds that "cannot be changed" because they are fixed on trusting their God. They're like photographs—fixed forever at a certain point. So, why do they "stubbornly" trust? Because the Lord is "an everlasting rock," the one who never changes and can, therefore, always be trusted.

If it seems that you have been pressured to change your mind about trusting in the Lord, now is the time to set your trust in Him again. Yes, the world may change, but God's love and care for you never will. So before going to sleep tonight, take a few moments to focus on God and choose to trust in Him again. When you have your mind set on one thing above all others—trusting God—you will experience a perfect peace that comes from heaven.

*Darkness now covers the earth, and thick darkness covers the
nations. But the LORD dawns, and his glory appears over you.*
Isaiah 60:2

Light in the Darkness

Storms at night seem to hold more menace. Some of the
worst storms in history—Hurricane Katrina, for example—
have taken place at night. Even though nightfall already eclipses the
light, the added layer of darkness seems to add to the oppression. Is
it any wonder that a lighthouse is such a symbol of hope during such
a stormy time? You can just picture the beam of light piercing the
gloom and helping a storm-tossed ship to navigate to safety.

In Isaiah 60:2, the prophet Isaiah talks about a different sort of
darkness: spiritual darkness. After predicting the future exile of the
people of Israel, Isaiah then contrasts the glory of the Lord, which the
people of Israel were to reflect, with the darkness of the earth. While
Israel often failed to reflect God's glory (hence the exile), God would
show them great mercy. Through them would come the ultimate
light—the Messiah. This light would pierce the darkness—showing
the way to God.

What storms have come your way? Perhaps you feel misun-
derstood, confused about an event in your life, or fearful about an
outcome. Perhaps you even question God's concern for your life. If so,
consider the message of this verse from Isaiah. The glory of the Lord
as embodied in Jesus, "the light of the world" (John 8:12), illuminates
the darkness. No darkness can conquer you, because He is your
keeper.

Lord,

as I sleep tonight, please calm
my fears and remind me of Your
presence in and with me. I give
my cares to You and trust You to
provide hope and clarity where
confusion reigns.

You are present in every season of my life, God. As I come to You tonight, I know that You understand what I am experiencing. Please grant to me your peace and the reassurance that You are always with me as I fall asleep.

If any of you are having trouble, pray.
If you are happy, sing psalms.
James 5:13

Every Season

Every one of us will go through different seasons in life—seasons of joy, seasons of sorrow, seasons of trouble, seasons of rest. How we relate to God during those different seasons in life will change as we are shaped by the events of a season. This verse in James acknowledges these differences and even instructs us how to react when we face different seasons.

How are you feeling tonight? Whether you are happy or sad, exuberant or troubled, you can always come to God. If you are troubled tonight, you may find it hard to sing songs of praise. God understands. You can pray in your trouble, though, even if all you can do is ask God for help and rest. He will hear you—and you will not be in this season forever.

If you are full of happiness tonight, sing your joy to God. He loves your voice and created you to praise Him with your lips. So whether you turn music on and sing along to praise songs or create a song in your heart for God, delight in Him and His goodness toward you. He is worthy of our praise!

God knows your heart and longs to connect with you, whether through prayer or song. Take some time to connect with God in the way that expresses your heart to Him tonight, and sleep with the deep peace of a woman who knows her Maker.

Come to me, all who are tired from carrying
heavy loads, and I will give you rest.
Matthew 11:28

Set Free!

You know what it's like to feel bone weary. At the end of a hard day, all you want to do is sink into a chair or lie down. But too often, exhaustion is a constant companion. Tired from the events of busy days, you slip into bed feeling the weight of the world on your shoulders. Not only are you bone weary physically but also emotionally. There are always more things to be done, and there never seem to be enough hours in the day to complete the tasks in front of you. You look to sleep to escape the heavy problems that you carry.

Thankfully, Jesus tells you that you do not have to carry these burdens on your own. He calls you to Himself, declaring that when you are tired from shouldering too much in your life, He will give you the rest that you need. More than just sleep, the rest that Christ offers is a rest for your soul (Matthew 11:29), one that refreshes you from the inside out.

Before your head hits the pillow tonight, take some time to tell Jesus about the burdens that are weighing you down emotionally, physically, and spiritually. Then, ask Him for the rest that He offers. You can fall asleep trusting Him to refresh and renew your soul.

Lord,
help me rest this evening
as I give You my hopes
and dreams. Forgive me
when I doubt You. O Lord,
increase my faith. Thank
You for the vastness of
Your universe. Remind
me that Your blessings
are as numerous as the
stars.

Lord God,

I really need Your help to guard my heart. There are so many distractions and so many fears that crowd You out sometimes. Set up spiritual precautions in my life so that I might not stray from You, the One who is worthy of my whole heart.

Guard your heart more than anything else, because the
source of your life flows from it.
Proverbs 4:23

Guard Your Heart

What flows from your heart? Praise? Complaints? Often-times, the deepest desires of our hearts come out as we prepare to sleep. In the Bible, the heart is often used as a metaphor for the core of a person's personality. It is our "source of life." Our actions and thoughts begin at our source, which is our hearts. And that is precisely why the wise writer Solomon told his sons to guard their hearts. Because the heart is the source of life, it needs to be protected from all that would potentially pollute it.

Jesus says that "your heart will be where your treasure is" (Matthew 6:21). Whatever we set our hearts on becomes the treasure—the priority or focus—of our lives. If we claim God as the source of our lives, that means He is the highest priority of our lives. Everything—the relationships we form, the activities we choose, the images we view—flows from that source. Thus, He invites us to guard our hearts from the pollution of worldly ideas and actions. We can do this by saying no to certain images or thoughts and saying yes to sources that accord with God's viewpoint.

Starting tonight, determine to guard your heart. The good news is that you don't have to go it alone. The Holy Spirit is with you to help safeguard His home—your heart. The best way to begin guarding your heart is to give it fully to Him.

The sun has one kind of splendor, the moon has another kind of splendor, and the stars have still another kind of splendor. Even one star differs in splendor from another star.
1 Corinthians 15:41

Splendor All Around

Paul wrote to the people of Corinth to inspire them with the glory promised to Christ's followers. As they struggled with the notion of a resurrected body, the Corinthians probably wondered whether or not their sick, aging bodies would continue troubling them in heaven.

Perhaps you have the same question tonight as you consider aches of the day. The images of splendor that Paul provides can be reassuring. Heaven means perfection. The body you will have in eternity will never grow old. In fact, the promise of resurrection is that you will be lit with splendor and experience a new kind of freedom. It's like the leaves of the hollyhock. They may look rough and unappealing as the plant grows, but nothing compares to the beauty of the flowers.

There is a purpose and a plan to this universe! Tonight you can look out your windows to see how the night sky shimmers with wonder. If God showers such beauty and abundance on the fields and in the sky, He must love you dearly.

Such a wonderful pattern you have to ponder. The world has been painted with designs to remind you—day follows night, freedom from pain comes with sleep, and the resurrection will bring splendor that will last throughout eternity.

Lord,

all I need to do is look
around to see how You
have blessed us with beauty
and wonder. I can't imagine
what heaven is like, but it
must be truly awesome.

Almighty God,

I need the rest that You
offer. Help me. In the
quiet of this night I surrender to You.

> *This is what the Almighty LORD, the Holy One of Israel, says: You can be saved by returning to me. You can have rest. You can be strong by being quiet and by trusting me.*
> Isaiah 30:15

Curl Up and Rest

A small baby curled up in the crib. Your dog or cat sprawled on the rug, sound asleep. What a picture of rest.

The prophet Isaiah describes another picture of rest: the security and peace inherent in placing the full weight of one's trust in God. Repentance was the step to attaining this security. However, the people of Judah clung to their old ways or repeatedly looked for help from other nations instead of trusting God.

God invites you to put the whole weight of your trust in Him as well and indulge in toe-curling rest. Even when you stray, God gives you opportunities to turn back to Him again and again. And what's more—He will give you rest, peace and comfort. He'll give you everything you need to get through the tribulations of your life.

Isn't it reassuring to know that you don't have to muster up superhuman strength to fight all of life's battles? Instead you can turn now, this very night, to God. When you quiet your mind and place your trust in Him, rest comes easily. You can curl up and let go of all your troubles because the source of strength is here. In the stillness of the night, turn to the Holy One.

When you look for me, you will find me. When you wholeheartedly seek me, I will let you find me, declares the LORD.
Jeremiah 29:13–14

Hide-and-Seek

Remember playing hide-and-seek as a kid? The shivering excitement of hiding and seeking is great as the game goes, but not so fun when the game becomes reality. For example, when answers to prayer seem a long time in coming, we sometimes feel as if God is hiding from us just as we're seeking Him.

Nevertheless, the Old Testament prophet Jeremiah provides an assurance of God's willingness to be found. If we seek God wholeheartedly, we will find Him—sometimes in unexpected ways. He can be discovered in the elegance of a sunset, the flickering of a candle flame, and in the gentle breeze coming through the window. And He can be discovered even closer than that. When we truly seek, we will hear the quiet voice of the Holy Spirit inside us. He has been waiting all this time to be found! The key is to keep seeking Him. As Jesus later said, "The one who searches will find, and for the one who knocks, the door will be opened" (Matthew 7:8).

Tonight as you pray, consider the ways God has guided you to this point in your life. Recalling the times of His intervention in your life is a little bit like playing hide-and-seek. Can you find God in your life? He's not hard to find, because He wants you to be found. What a comfort that is.

A Lord,

I see You in all the wonders around me. How wonderful it is to discover You anew. Help me to look for You in everything and to say "thank You" at each new discovery. Help me know You better.

Lord,

I'm grateful that I'm not
alone. Your strength is
my strength. You are my
family and my comfort.
Thank You.

I will not leave you all alone. I will come back to you.
John 14:18

Never Alone

Nighttime often stirs up feelings of loneliness. With the darkness blanketing everything and everyone, we feel isolated, especially if we're the only one awake in the house. But wakefulness isn't only an isolator. It is often an indicator of unresolved problems, fears, and other worries. We feel all alone in our anguish.

If you experienced such a feeling recently, you can understand how Jesus' disciples felt when their beloved Master announced His upcoming death. The One they walked with, ate with, and poured their lives into would be gone. But Jesus also promised that they wouldn't be left alone. Not only would Jesus return from the dead, He also would send the Holy Spirit to be with them always.

Although the disciples couldn't quite grasp Jesus' words at the time, His resurrection (John 20) and the sending of the Holy Spirit (Acts 2) showed that Jesus kept His promise.

This promise is for you as well. Even when you feel troubled and alone, Jesus promises that you are never truly alone. You have the assurance of the Holy Spirit's presence, guidance, comfort, and strength.

Tonight you can rest in the Spirit who surrounds you with love and promises never to leave you. Thanks to the Holy Spirit, you'll never walk alone.

O LORD my God, I have taken refuge in you. Save me,
and rescue me from all who are pursuing me.
Psalm 7:1

Rescue Me

Sometimes an endless tirade of guilt or recriminations plays in our heads. We toss and turn with messages like *I said the wrong thing. I'm worthless. My mistakes are unforgivable.* At other times the tirade includes the remarks or opinions of others—opinions that rob us of our sleep or cause us to beat ourselves up.

David, the author of this psalm, was accused of trying to steal Saul's throne. While the accusation was untrue, David suffered for it with Saul's relentless pursuit. Rather than seeking revenge, he turned to God for relief.

What is the safest place you can think of? Is it a mountain castle or fortress? Or is your place of refuge someplace closer to home, like a basement—your retreat when storms brew outside? As David explained, there is no safer place than God. He is the ultimate refuge.

The Father's loving arms are stretched out waiting for you to run to Him. When you are in need of a salve for your heart, all you have to do is rush to Him and surrender your life into His powerful care. Like a life preserver, He surrounds you and lifts you to safety.

Surrender isn't a bad thing in this case. It means going to the One who is stronger and wiser and saying, "I need You." Through prayer you can give your doubts to Him. Then in the safety of His arms, the accusations cease. With untroubled thoughts, sleep comes readily.

I run to You

for help, dear Father.
Please silence the accusa-
tions that torment me.
The world is filled with
injustice and pain, but
You are my loving Father.
I surrender to You.

Lord,

when I have faced times
of trouble, You have been
my help and my light. My
arms will not grow tired
of being lifted up to You.
The comfort I seek comes
in knowing that You are
listening.

On the day I was in trouble, I went to the Lord for help. At night I stretched out my hands in prayer without growing tired. Yet, my soul refused to be comforted.

Psalm 77:2

Shifting Gears

Picture it: you've just had a hard day, a day in which you heard some devastating news. You come home and your family tries to cheer you up or comfort you in some way. Could you accept the comfort extended?

When Asaph, the writer of Psalm 77, found himself in anguish, he turned to a tried and true source of comfort: God. Yet he still found himself comfortless. By the end of Psalm 77, however, he came to a feeling of acceptance. Meditating on "the deeds of the Lord" (77:11) helped him shift gears.

When you stop seeing God and get stuck in a world of personal troubles, it's hard to find peace of mind. The answer is to switch gears. But this is easier said than done. It can be difficult to shift from your disappointments and expectations to seeing how God works for good.

As you prepare for bed this evening, make that transition from worry to peace by focusing on images of God. Consider how many wonderful people God has brought into your life. How many opportunities has God given you to learn and grow? You can cultivate a feeling of gratitude, and this will lead to courage and change.

To prepare for sleep tonight, try to release your troubles. Shift the focus from me to He. May you then find comfort.

Let my prayer be accepted as sweet-smelling incense in your presence. Let the lifting up of my hands in prayer be accepted as an evening sacrifice.
Psalm 141:2

Rise Up, My Soul

For hundreds of years, incense has accompanied prayer on its journey to God. Wafts of white smoke curl and dance toward the ceiling. As it rises, the smoke symbolically lifts the prayers out of this earthly realm.

David, the writer of Psalm 141, well knew the use of incense in worship. It was a fit metaphor for his desperate plea, which flowed like the smoke of the incense.

The rising smoke also is an image of our faith. It defies gravity by rising heavenward instead of falling back to earth. When we lift our hands and voices toward God, we defy logic too. While an unbelieving person might say there is no physical presence in the room to hear us, we trust that God hears each word.

Your prayers merge with the prayers of others like whiffs of smoke. You ask for forgiveness for yourself or for others. You offer thanks. You ask for help for your troubled world. You seek guidance.

Tonight, you can make a simple ritual by lighting a candle while you pray. After you pray, blow out the candle and watch the smoke rise. As it rises, your soul will rise up with it, to meet your loving Savior.

❧ *Father,*

I send my prayers to You,
enveloped in the sweet
smell of incense. As the
smoke drifts upward, I
feel my soul lifting up
as well. Thank You for
helping me rise above my
day-to-day problems to
trust that You are here.
You are taking care of
everything.

Lord, calm my heart. Quiet my soul. Open my ears so that I might recognize Your voice. Make me ready and willing to follow at Your beckoning.

*Samuel was asleep in the temple of the LORD where the ark of God was kept.
Then the LORD called Samuel. "Here I am," Samuel responded.*
1 Samuel 3:3–4

Are You Listening?

Daytime is often filled with noises and distractions. It is the time to go, accomplish, and check off the to-do list. But nighttime and its coveted hours meant for rest can be hampered with the replaying of these noises and distractions. Sometimes we're so busy replaying the day that we miss listening for "the quiet, whispering voice" of the Lord (1 Kings 19:12).

In 1 Samuel, the importance of an attitude of listening is revealed in an interaction between God and Samuel, a boy given by his mother Hannah to serve God at the tabernacle. One night, Samuel thought he heard someone call his name. Assuming it was Eli, he hurried to the priest's side. This happened three times. After Eli determined that God was calling Samuel, Eli suggested a humble response: "Speak, LORD. I'm listening" (1 Samuel 3:9).

How would you respond if the Lord called your name? Is your life so busy that you wouldn't be able to hear the Lord if He called you? Or would you recognize His voice like an infant recognizes her mother's soft inflection and touch?

God speaks through His Word, through the Holy Spirit, and through the wise counsel of others. His voice is like the quiet voice of a radio host tuned to the frequency of our hearts. Are you listening?

> *Remember your Creator when the doors to the street are closed, the sound of the mill is muffled, you are startled at the sound of a bird, and those who sing songs become quiet.*
> Ecclesiastes 12:4

Looking Back

What do you usually do when you're feeling nostalgic? Play old songs? Look at old photographs? A feeling of nostalgia often involves taking a glance in the rearview mirror of our lives. Captured images can remind us of a loved one, an event, or a fading memory. Sometimes the recollection is calming, especially if the memory evoked is a happy one.

The writer of Ecclesiastes encouraged a sense of nostalgia in regard to the Creator. At the beginning of the chapter, he encouraged the remembrance of God "when you are young" (12:1). In the rest of the chapter, the descending of night and the changes in season are symbolic of the aging process. In a sense he is saying "Remember the Creator throughout your life."

Meditating on your Creator—remembering His attributes and actions—is a discipline that can carry you through good and bad times. You can ready yourself for taxing moments by consistently preparing and praying. Preparing—reading the Word, seeking wise counsel—equips you as you go through life. If you are grounded in the comfortable moments, you will be more likely to stay grounded in the challenging ones, when it is so much easier to become jaded.

As you lie in bed, consider the ways your Creator made His presence known during your faith journey. How can you continue to equip yourself for a lifelong journey with Christ?

Lord,

place in me a desire to
study Your Word and
know You better in com-
fortable and challenging
times. Ready me for
moments when You are
quiet or when I am feel-
ing alone. Thank You for
never abandoning me.

Lord,

thank You for providing
moments of rest. I offer
You my daily schedule to
allow You to take priority
over all other details and
distractions.

He will say to them, "This is a place for comfort. This is a place of
rest for those who are tired. This is a place for them to rest."
Isaiah 28:12

A Place of Rest

You've spent a very busy day. You've worked hard. You've handled your share of excitement, joy, sorrow, crises—you name it. The day is over and now it's time to rest.

What if you decided you weren't going to rest? What if you said that you wanted to keep going, keep working through the night and into the next day? Eventually, your body would overrule and you would collapse into much needed sleep. Your body knows that you need rest in order to keep up with your responsibilities.

The context of the verse in Isaiah comes as God was speaking to His people in the northern kingdom of Israel. They had sinned greatly. The last phrase of the verse above (not quoted) is "but they weren't willing to listen." Isaiah reminded the people that God had given them the land of Canaan in which to rest, but they took Him for granted and rejected His provision. They had other plans; they wanted to go their own way.

Today's world offers an endless supply of activities and opportunities. When you allow your daily routines to define, control, and deplete you, however, it is an indication that reprioritization is needed. God wants you to rest when you're tired; He knows you need it. Which activities are preventing you from resting? Ask the Lord to help you slow down, reset your priorities, and find the rest that you need.

After all, tomorrow is a busy day.

Who among you fears the LORD and obeys his servant?
Let those who walk in darkness and have no light trust the
name of the LORD and depend upon their God.
Isaiah 50:10

Sensing God

The Lord has given us senses to detect Him. They are tools to know and follow Him. He gave us eyes to see the purple shades of sunsets, noses to smell the deep musk of autumn and lilac springs, ears to hear rain gently spilling onto roofs, tongues to taste fresh produce, and touch to feel the soft sand between our toes.

But isn't it interesting how in sudden dark situations, we feel cut off from some of our senses? The sudden blackout disorients us. Not only can't we see, we're often not sure we hear as well either!

Isaiah used darkness as a metaphor for times of turmoil. During those times when we're tempted to panic or doubt our senses, Isaiah champions a dependence on God. Only He can see all sides of a situation. So, instead of flailing about in the darkness of our misunderstanding, we are to trust in the presence of God. The Holy Spirit is like a spiritual compass—one that always points us in the right direction.

As you lie in bed tonight, focus on each of your senses and how they may be used to acknowledge the Lord and strengthen your faith. Revisit your day. When did you use your senses to recognize the Lord or to further the Kingdom? In what tangible ways did He help you when you were tempted to doubt your senses?

Lord,

train my senses to
recognize You. Provide
opportunities to enjoy
and share Your creation
and promises with others.
When I lack understand-
ing about a situation,
guide me in the right
direction.

Lord,

I praise You for being bigger
than any concern or worry
I may experience in my life.
Teach me to lean on You
when I become anxious.

> *So don't ever worry about tomorrow. After all, tomorrow will worry*
> *about itself. Each day has enough trouble of its own.*
> Matthew 6:34

Make-Believe

An old pair of high heels, one of grandmother's fancy party hats, and a mismatched collection of bangle bracelets beckon most little girls into whimsical fairy tales, imaginary worlds, and fantastic daydreams. Cares and concerns, although seemingly simple in childhood, are whisked away as each bracelet slips over a tiny wrist and an elegant lady, bedecked in costume jewelry, emerges. No adventure is out of bounds, no dream impossible. Reality will wait until costumes and jewelry are returned to their cluttered toy trunk at the end of the day.

As today comes to an end, which aspects of reality and its trials surface and consume you? Do you wish that an assortment of once-polished bracelets could be slipped on, allowing you to escape to that perfectly painted setting? Take heart. In Christ, dress-up clothes or an escape into fantasy are not necessary for solace. Instead, He offers true solace by cautioning His followers to avoid worrying about what will happen tomorrow. This is not a bury-your-head-in-the-sand piece of advice, but an invitation to lay your worries and burdens down at His feet. As the Lord points out, "Can any of you add a single hour to your life by worrying?" (Matthew 6:27). Instead, you can trust in the Lord; trust in His promises. His faithfulness will never lose its luster.

He makes me lie down in green pastures. He leads me
beside peaceful waters. He renews my soul.
Psalm 23:2-3

A Renewed Soul

As you sit down in the evening and exhale that deep, end-of-day exhalation, imagine yourself sitting on the edge of a wooden dock at sunset. You experience creation's quiet magnificence. When you dip your toes into the calming water, weariness is eased and rest is found. When the sultry breeze brushes through your hair and you listen to the ebbing tide breaking across the shore, peace is found. When your eyes follow the setting sun's golden trail across the water's glassy surface and into the hills, restoration is found.

The Lord desires rest and restoration for His children. David, the one-time shepherd turned king of Israel, recognized God as a shepherd who cares for His flock. He commands us to, "Let go of your concerns! Then you will know that I am God" (Psalm 46:10). Christ provides us with settings that promise stillness. He guides us into havens that encourage comfort. He desires us to seek and secure moments of rest so that our souls might be renewed. A tranquil soul is a soul that is capable of serving and worshiping the Creator.

As you lie in bed tonight, ask the Lord to quiet your soul so that you might reflect on Him and wake rested and revitalized tomorrow.

A Heavenly Father,

thank You for revealing Yourself in nature. Quiet my soul so that I might recognize You in the world around me.

Lord,

teach me to seek refuge
in You when I am afraid.
Guide me each day with
Your Word and through
the Holy Spirit.

He will cover you with his feathers, and under his wings you will find refuge. His truth is your shield and armor. You do not need to fear terrors of the night, arrows that fly during the day, plagues that roam the dark.
Psalm 91:4–6

Tucked In

For children, nighttime often inspires a range of far-fetched notions and menacing fears, some of which are alleviated when a parent arrives to tuck them in and assure them that everything is okay. For adults, dark shadows no longer unleash a fury of monsters and apprehensions, but life's day-to-day challenges do. Sickness, financial instability, job struggles, concern for children—these occur day and night. We long for someone to take away our fears or pain—to tuck us in, so to speak, with words of comfort.

Can you relate? If so, consider the message of Psalm 91 and its vivid images of protection and provision. We need not fear the trials of this life because God, who is our protection and harbor, covers us. He has given us the Holy Spirit to dwell inside us as we learn and grow from the challenges we encounter. He also has given us His Word as a guide to truth.

As you crawl into bed at night, contemplate the ways in which the Lord looks after you. Perhaps He provided wise counsel at just the right time. Or, perhaps He flooded you with peace as you waited for the doctor's diagnosis. Tonight, allow the truth of His love for you to tuck you in. You can rest assured under His wings.

Now that we have God's approval by faith, we have peace
with God because of what our Lord Jesus Christ has done.
Romans 5:1

Seal of Approval

Human approval is often based on certain conditions being met. A person might gain our approval through obedience or by possessing a trait we admire (beauty, goodness, success, fame, independence of thought, high intellect). We withhold our approval if the conditions we've set are not met.

In the letter to the Romans, the apostle Paul describes another kind of approval—God's. We can't earn it by being "good." Instead, God approves us "because of what Jesus Christ has done." This means that because of Jesus' perfect fulfillment of every letter of the law and especially His sacrificial death on the cross, we are no longer at war with God. Jesus' resurrection sealed the deal and ushered in a new era of peace with God.

Tonight, consider who or what gains your seal of approval. What are the times when you're most tempted to believe that you don't have God's approval? If your faith has been shaken recently because of a hardship, meditate on Paul's words. Consider also these words from Paul: "I am convinced that nothing can ever separate us from God's love which Christ Jesus our Lord shows us" (Romans 8:38).

Tonight as you close your eyes, consider the amazing fact that you have God's seal of approval.

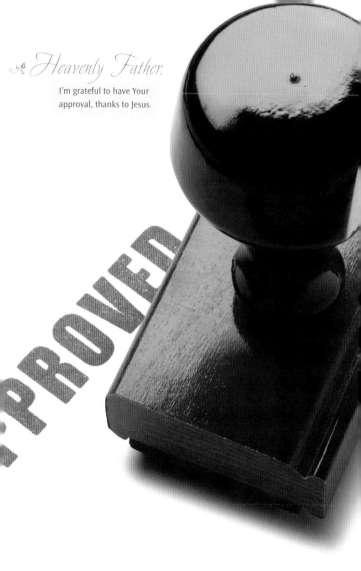

Heavenly Father,

I'm grateful to have Your
approval, thanks to Jesus.

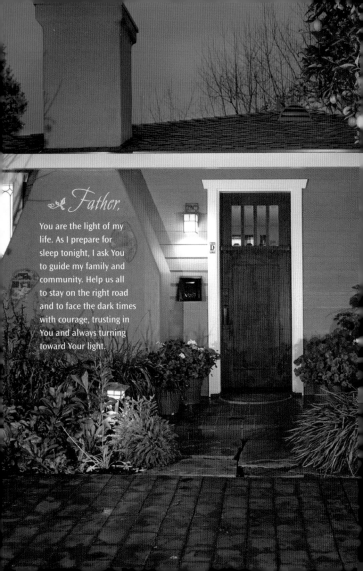

Father,

You are the light of my life. As I prepare for sleep tonight, I ask You to guide my family and community. Help us all to stay on the right road and to face the dark times with courage, trusting in You and always turning toward Your light.

> *There will be no more night, and they will not need any*
> *light from lamps or the sun because the Lord God will shine*
> *on them. They will rule as kings forever and ever.*
> *Revelation 22:5*

Journeying Home

Have you ever dreamed about taking a trip to a distant, exotic place? Most of us know what this is like. We long for the opportunity to see new places, to experience something different. We know such a trip will refresh and renew us.

Could you imagine your own home being a place of refreshment as well as exciting and exotic? Your true home—heaven—is. We have hints of what this special destination will be like from the book of Revelation. According to the vision of the apostle John, it is a place of wonderful illumination. Our eyes will be able to feast on beautiful golden light. All truth and all reality will be clear. We will be with the King and live as kings. And there will be no more death, no more darkness, no more fear. Such a bountiful place of perfection and purity it will be!

The light of heaven trickles down into our lives now. When we're confused about choices or challenges, God provides "light" through His Word to guide us (Psalm 119:105; Ephesians 1:18).

As you prepare for sleep tonight, consider what excites you the most about this awesome heavenly home. If you've spent all day in the hot sun or worried about paying your electric bill, perhaps the thought of never needing another lamp might fill you with longing. If so, that's great! This dream becomes a beacon during your journey on earth. Like a spotlight, it points the way home.

> *Let Christ's peace control you. God has called you into this*
> *peace by bringing you into one body. Be thankful.*
> Colossians 3:15

A Purpose for Peace

Imagine the feeling of being welcomed home by close family and friends after a long trip. Feel the familiar embraces. See the genuine smiles. Hear the tender voices. This is the intimacy that Christ desires for us among our Christian brothers and sisters. This is the feeling of being part of a whole—one that will carry over in heaven.

We are instructed to love one another (Matthew 22:39; John 13:35). The Lord has called us to live in peace with others, reflecting His love. Sadly, some of our interchanges are characterized by arguments, rather than peace. We snipe and gripe, dwell on misunderstandings, or fall into judgmental thoughts of others. Churches have split and relationships have ended over such misunderstandings. Knowing of human nature, Paul included the above admonition to encourage his readers to be controlled by the Holy Spirit—the author of peace and the One who connects all believers. If we allow the Lord's peace to control our tongues and tempers, we will be a reflection of Him.

Perhaps tonight you're in need of peace. There is no better time than now to ask for it.

 *Lord God,*

grant me the patience and
humility necessary to forgive
and love fully. Surround me with
community and fellowship, so
that I might be part of one body.

Dear Lord,

I praise You for Your un-
conditional love and grace.
Guard me from lies that may
cause me to feel inadequate
and hesitant to approach
You. Help me to grasp the
extent of Your mercy.

We can go to God with bold confidence through faith in Christ.
Ephesians 3:12

As You Are

Ever think of yourself as limited in some way—too limited to be of use to God? If you feel you lack attributes or resources that others have (higher education; a nice house; a sizable bank account; eloquence in speech and other abilities) or if you've made mistakes in the past, you can't imagine being used by God to build His kingdom. Yet consider the fact that the apostle Paul wrote the letter to the Ephesians while imprisoned in Rome. Little did he know that he would have a great impact for the Kingdom during this time.

Although he was a prisoner, Paul considered his position a privilege. After all, he had been chosen by God to share His Good News. And that's the whole point, isn't it—being chosen by God to do the work to which you are called? For this very reason, you can approach the Lord confidently, knowing that His mercies extend to all those who believe the Gospel.

Consider the way in which you approach the Lord. Do you come cautiously or boldly? As Paul declares, you can draw near the Lord unencumbered—much like a simple sunflower, exposed and concentrated on the vast heavens above. You can bring your burdens and shortcomings to Christ, knowing that His unconditional love and grace are not just for the sinless and blameless. His love and grace are meant for everyone. As today comes to a close, come to the Lord just as you are.

Jesus Christ is the same yesterday, today, and forever.
Hebrews 13:8

Telling Time

The longcase clock, also known as a grandfather clock, has been a symbol of time since its advent in 1670. You can count on it to chime the quarter hour, half hour, and the hour. Tick. Tock. Gong . . . gong . . . gong. The clock indicates the passage of time, and change is time's companion.

Whether or not invited, unexpected twists and turns permeate our lives. As the old saying goes, change is the only constant in this world. Relationships go through seasons of change, jobs change, and disasters sometimes trigger unexpected changes. This is the nature of a temporary world.

Perhaps tonight you're contemplating or reeling from an unexpected change. If so, take heart. The writer of Hebrews declares that Jesus will never change. When all else seems uncertain, rest assured that our Savior was and is and will forever be constant. We can find trust in and rely on Him, knowing that His promises to us will not falter.

Take a moment to quietly reflect on cherished memories that have remained constant in your life from year to year. Is it the family's chiming grandfather clock in the hallway? Is it a tradition that takes place each holiday season? What remains unchanged, providing a sense of comfort and familiarity? Praise God for the constants and for His presence in every season of life.

Heavenly Father,

I'm grateful for Your unwavering love and grace. Teach me to trust You in times of uncertainty.

Father,

thank You for being in control
and for Your master plan.
Teach me to trust in You and to
abandon the security I seek in
my own abilities.

Trust the LORD with all your heart, and do not rely on your own understanding. In all your ways acknowledge him, and he will make your paths smooth.
Proverbs 3:5–6

Smooth Sailing

Envision yourself deep in the Rockies. All is still and silent. Even the mischievous wind has bedded down for a rest along the narrow path. Not far ahead, a clearing appears amid the evergreens' deep shade. As you emerge, the setting sun reveals a stunning, nearly glowing landscape of white. A thick layer of pristine snow subtly glimmers across the mountain and from every bowing branch lining the slope. In the distance, snow-capped peaks pierce the orange and indigo sky. You move into the opening, and the fresh air nips at your cheeks and floods your body. In front of you, stillness extends, your path freer and smoother than flight.

Now imagine a hang glider launching off one of the rocky cliffs. Could you do that? Even if you couldn't physically do it, God invites you to hang glide spiritually, in a sense, by putting the full weight of your trust in Him as you take a step of faith. When we rely on our own strength, we confine ourselves to a lonely and aimless life, marked by uncertain and dangerous turns. When we acknowledge the Lord and His teachings, we glide on His strength and His resolve. These paths will take unexpected turns at times, but with Christ as our guide, we can confidently anticipate and travel the adventures ahead.

Tonight, consider the path before you. Perhaps you're contemplating a change the Lord is nudging you to make. Are you willing to "trust the Lord with all your heart"?

The eternal God is your shelter, and his everlasting arms
support you. He will force your enemies out of your way
and tell you to destroy them.
Deuteronomy 33:27

Living a Sheltered Life

Shelter is one of the fundamental needs of human beings. Most of us think of our home as our shelter—a place where we feel safe and protected from harm, especially at night when the doors are locked and the shades drawn. Shelter comes in many forms—whether it's a tent for climbers in the Rockies, or a house on stilts in the Amazon River basin, an igloo, or even a mud hut. People around the globe create a shelter from the materials around them in order to live safe from the elements.

Today's passage contains some final words Moses spoke to the Israelites. Soon they would leave the wilderness for the Promised Land. Moses understood their fear of the future, of facing unknown enemies. He gave them a message of hope, assuring them of God's protection and provision as they sheltered in His everlasting arms.

Your feelings may mimic those of the Israelites when they faced an unknown future. The potential for tragedy or turmoil in other ways can seem ever present, affecting our ability to sleep. When you think about the future, what comes to mind? Fearful thoughts? Uncertainty? If so, consider the shelter Moses discovered. Like the Israelites, you can relax in the shelter of God's everlasting arms and trust your future to Him.

Father,

I can't control my future.
But I can trust in You
to be my shelter when
I place my life in Your
everlasting arms. Through
the security I find in You,
give me a sound sleep
tonight I pray.

Father,

as I worship You in song,
may I surrender to sleep.

> *But no one asks, "Where is God, my Creator, who inspires songs in the night, who teaches us more than he teaches the animals of the earth, who makes us wiser than the birds in the sky?"*
>
> Job 35:10–11

Inspiration

It's bedtime. You should be sleepy, but you're just not able to relax. Your brain's busy mulling over tomorrow's to-do list, and you can't settle down. So what puts you in a restful mood? Reading a chapter or two? Listening to your favorite CDs? What is your music of choice? Country music? Pop? Gospel? Classical?

Elihu, a friend of Job, suggested another type of music—songs inspired by God. While the Bible is not specific on the types of songs imagined by Elihu, we can't help thinking of the songs of the Bible: the Psalms.

Tucked under the covers, reading a bedtime devotional that describes God's ability to "inspire songs in the night," perhaps you're wondering, Can God really do that for me, even if I'm struggling financially? Having problems with my boss? Coping with my mother's serious health issues?

Your life does not have to be 100 percent perfect before God can give you a song in the night. If you look back at the Psalms, you will see that life wasn't at all rosy for many psalmists. Yet they acknowledged that God was still good, even when life was at its worst. Turn your thoughts toward God. Revel in His presence, His love, His care. Hum a favorite hymn. And fall to sleep.

> *I will praise the LORD, who advises me. My conscience*
> *warns me at night. I always keep the LORD in front of me.*
> *When he is by my side, I cannot be moved.*
> *Psalm 16:7–8*

I Cannot Be Moved

The words "I cannot be moved" from the Scripture might seem familiar because they are used in the hymn "I Shall Not Be Moved." Many children are taught this song. However, in a child's understanding, the meaning behind the lyrics must seem obscure. What kind of spiritual significance is found in the words "I shall not be moved"?

The words are full of determination—the will, the resolve, the intent to stay put. In Psalm 16, David, who had the reputation of being a man after God's own heart (1 Samuel 13:14), explained his resolve to cling to God. Instead of trusting in his weapons or his soldiers, he placed the full weight of his trust in God's protection, knowing that nothing could move him with an immovable God at his side. Centuries later, Jesus would encourage His followers to do the same (John 15:4–8).

He wants that same "I cannot be moved" response from you. His constant availability gives you the opportunity to communicate with Him all day every day—and all night as well! He offers you advice through His Word and His Spirit. He's ready to respond to your questions, your prayers, and your concerns anytime.

As you tuck the covers under your chin, remind yourself of David's assurance, "Complete joy is in your presence. Pleasures are by your side forever" (Psalm 16:11).

O Lord,

I commit to standing by
Your side so that Your
closeness will prevent
anything from moving me
away from Your presence.

Lord,

I offer You my burdens tonight. Help me to forgive and release the load to You and accept Your peace.

Turn your burdens over to the LORD, and he will take care of you. He will never let the righteous person stumble.
Psalm 55:22

Load Carrier

Before the invention of cars and trucks and trains, explorers and traders often used horses, donkeys, and mules as pack animals to carry their equipment and goods across unknown territory. Traditional pack animals in other regions of the world include llamas, Bactrian camels, dromedary camels, yaks, elephants, water buffalos, dogs, and reindeer. Every animal carries its load on its back in some style of backpack.

Let's be honest. You probably don't associate with pack-carrying beasts of burden in your daily schedule. But perhaps you're a burden-bearer yourself—burdens of the emotional kind. David, one of the ancient kings of Israel, knew all about burdens.

When David wrote Psalm 55, he was dealing with the burden of betrayal, having been double-crossed by someone he trusted. In his suffering, David recognized the One who could help him carry his burden of anguish, grief, and despair—his Lord. Consequently, he encouraged all to "turn your burdens over to the LORD."

What are your burdens? If you're carrying around a purse full of painful burdens tonight (and even a stylish purse doesn't make the burden any lighter), know that you don't have to bear the weight alone. The Lord is ever present and ready to assist you and take care of you. As you pray, take time to name each one. Let Him lighten your load.

Like the moon his throne will stand firm forever. It will be
like a faithful witness in heaven.
Psalm 89:37

Moonstruck

When you step outside into a dark, clear night, there's a chance you'll look up at the stars and scan the sky, searching for the moon. A full moon engulfs you with its powerful magnetism, its beauty, its promise of romance.

The phases of the moon remain as predictable now as they were thousands of years ago. That's why the moon was the perfect metaphor for King David's dynasty. After rejecting David's offer to build a temple, God made a covenant with David concerning his descendants (2 Samuel 7:11-16). Not only would David's son ascend the throne, but centuries later, a Messiah would come from David's family's line. This Messiah—Jesus—will be King forever.

This passage also is a tribute to God's faithfulness in bringing about His promises. His love and faithfulness work together. He doesn't spoon out His love one bite at a time nor does He measure your love for Him and match His love to that equation. Instead, He freely offers the full measure of His love to each person.

Are you unsure about God's love for you? You can fix that tonight before you fall to sleep. Close your eyes and call His name. Confess any doubts you might have. Then cling to Him, for He promises to respond when He hears your call. Like the moon, His throne will stand firm forever.

Lord,

like the moon Your love
will stand forever like
a faithful witness in
heaven. My heart is Your
earthly throne. When I'm
tempted to doubt, renew
my faith in You.

Lord,

when I follow Your directions I don't get lost. Help me recognize the ways You are guiding me.

Your word is a lamp for my feet and a light for my path.
Psalm 119:105

Seeking the Light

What is your favorite source when you need directions? The GPS in your car or phone? MapQuest? The atlas tucked under the seat of your car? Your grandfather's compass? The more trusted the source, the better.

The writer of Psalm 119 invites you to consider a source of direction that many trust. Psalm 119, the longest psalm in the Bible, catalogues the ways that God's Word—His laws and decrees—directs our paths.

Consider the stories in the Bible of people exposed to the light of God literally and figuratively. God appeared as a pillar of fire to guide the people of Israel to the Promised Land (Exodus 13:21–22). Jesus described Himself as the "light of the world" (John 8:12). Saul of Tarsus experienced a dramatic encounter with the "light of the world" on the road to Damascus (Acts 9). God appeared as a burning bush to Moses (Exodus 3). But Psalm 119:105 refers to God's light as God's revelation—His revealing of who He is and how He works through His creation.

Perhaps tonight you're in need of illumination in the midst of a confusing situation. Open God's Word. It is a lamp for your feet and a light for your path, allowing you to walk carefully without fear of falling. Know that even when you turn out the light to sleep, you can rest in the promise of God's light.

What do people get from all of their hard work and struggles under the sun?
Their entire life is filled with pain, and their work is unbearable. Even at
night their minds don't rest. Even this is pointless.
Ecclesiastes 2:22–23

From God's Hand

Some might ask themselves, "Why did I bother?" when a frustrating outcome is the result of hours or years of hard effort. For example, when you spent hours cleaning the house for a family gathering only to find your efforts criticized or undermined by others trashing the house. Or, if you spent years chasing after a dream only to have the dream become a nightmare. This realization sadly turns to bitterness or disillusionment.

Perhaps you're feeling like that right now. The writer of Ecclesiastes isn't telling you to adopt a "why bother" attitude, even though he alludes to some activities as pointless. Worrying about matters totally outside the realm of your control or spending your whole life chasing after satisfaction outside of the will of God is like trying to sweep the sand off the beach—pointless. But just one verse later, he leads us to the right attitude: "There is nothing better for people to do than to eat, drink, and find satisfaction in their work. I saw that even this comes from the hand of God" (Ecclesiastes 2:24). Note that satisfaction comes "from the hand of God."

You have access to a heavenly Father who craves your friendship and obedience to His ways. In return, He allows joy and peace to saturate your spirit. Turn your mind to Him as you settle into bed this evening. Allow yourself to be comforted by His Spirit. Smile. Now slide into your night of sleep.

Father,

knowing You brings
meaning to my life.
Help me to focus on the
aspects of my life that are
important to You. May my
trust in You bring rest to
me tonight.

Lord,

I hand my tomorrow over to You. May I be filled with Your joy and peace tonight.

Let godly people triumph in glory.
Let them sing for joy on their beds.
Psalm 149:5

Counting Sheep

The search for a good night's sleep began long ago. Ancient Persians improved the quality of their sleep by using goatskins filled with water to make beds. The Romans stuffed cloth bags with wool, hay, or reeds—the wealthy preferred feather stuffing. In the sixteenth century, people built timber bed frames to hold their mattresses. The invention of the inner-spring mattress in 1871 by Heinrich Westphal led to softer, more comfortable beds.

Today mattress companies promise in their ads that their pillow-top mattresses, adjustable mattresses, or waterbeds will provide restful sleep. However, even if you sleep on a mattress that's built using the highest level of technology, you might still have nights when you're counting sheep in order to sleep. Sometimes the worries and frustrations of the day keep sleep at bay.

The first sentence of today's Scripture verse challenges you to approach sleep with a right attitude toward God. Recognizing His authority over all creatures and all creation as well as yourself and every aspect of your life can release you from that heaviness that interrupts your sleep. Do that and you will be able to follow the verse's pre-sleep pattern: Sing for joy on your bed. Thank God through songs of praise. Believe He is able to fill you with contentment and rest as you praise His name.

And you won't need to count sheep!

Forget what happened in the past, and do not dwell on events from long ago.
I am going to do something new. It is already happening. Don't you recognize
it? I will clear a way in the desert. I will make rivers on dry land.
Isaiah 43:18–19

The Oasis

t's not fun to remember "living in the desert" experiences—times of overpowering problems with undetermined solutions. Desert living makes your thirst for life evaporate as you analyze your choices for the future. It causes you to imagine a tomorrow that mimics past miserable situations with no guarantees of a better future.

The book of Isaiah gives some helpful advice straight out of the mouth of God. "Forget what happened in the past," says the Lord. But how can I forget about the past? you might ask yourself. Those times of severe thirst and dryness have left indelible marks. I can't shake off the memories.

You can stop focusing on the past and look to the future because of God's promise: "I am going to do something new. It is already happening." Take a look around you and purposefully search for signs of God's hand at work in your life. Remember how He answered past prayers to meet your specific needs. Dwell on how faithful He has been to uphold and guide you through previous difficult situations.

The God who, like an oasis, can "make rivers on dry land" promises to refresh you, encourage you, and enable you to live a life pleasing to Him. Walk into the cool water of His love and relax into a deep sleep tonight.

Dear God,

I accept Your love and
commit to being obedient
to Your guidance tonight.

Dear Lord,

thank You for being my hero.
As I give You my love and
accept Your peace, show me
ways to share Your love with
others.

The LORD your God is with you. He is a hero who saves
you. He happily rejoices over you, renews you with his love,
and celebrates over you with shouts of joy.
Zephaniah 3:17

Heroes

History is loaded with heroes and heroines. Florence Night-ingale was honored for revolutionizing nursing care during the Crimean War. Rosa Parks was respected for refusing to sit at the back of the bus at the beginnings of the Civil Rights movement, and Marie Curie admired for the discovery of radium and polonium. Or maybe your hero is that nurse at the ER who stayed with you through a difficult time.

Heroes often reflect similar traits: courage, determination, a desire for justice. That's why children love to pretend to be heroes. One compound word, however, sums up a hero's mandatory trait: self-sacrifice. They often face health problems, incarceration, life-threatening situations, or death for their causes.

How does God fit into the above description of heroes? That's easy. He gave His Son Jesus to save you from your sins. Jesus' sacrifice opened the door to God's love and makes a personal relationship with Him possible.

God rejoices when you accept His love, when you listen to His Spirit, when you talk to Him in prayer. As you prepare to sleep, allow your mind to dwell on the marvelous result of God's sacrifice—your relationship with Him. Ask Him to use that relationship to share His truth with the world. When you follow God's example of self-sacrifice, you will be a hero.

I've told you this so that my peace will be with you. In the world you'll have trouble. But cheer up! I have overcome the world.
John 16:33

The Peace Prize

Everybody enjoys wining a prize, even if the prize is not expensive. For example, the door prize at a meeting, the blue ribbon for the best flower in the garden show, or the clever gadget at the kitchenware party. Winning a prize brings a smile to your face and a jolt of excitement to your brain. However, there's one kind of prize that your hands don't hold. It's the peace that Jesus gives to those who love Him.

When Jesus says, "My peace will be with you," He's not promising you a trouble-free life. He's talking about providing you with peace of mind and heart. By trusting Jesus enough to turn your life over to Him and agreeing to follow His leading in your everyday activities, you open the door to His peace gift. Having His peace doesn't mean you'll quickly find the answers to all your problems. Instead, you'll have the assurance that Jesus is bigger than those problems and that He will help you find solutions because He proclaimed, "I have overcome the world."

This peace prize is available to you tonight. If fears or worries threaten your sleep, remember the peace Jesus offers. Close your eyes, and place your complete confidence in Him. Allow His peace to blanket you and go to sleep.

Dear Lord,

I am offering You the sacrifice of trust tonight. Give me Your peace, I pray.

Thank You,
Jesus, for guiding my life.
I am turning my difficul-
ties over to You tonight.

We take every thought captive so that it is obedient to Christ.
2 Corinthians 10:5

Every Thought

In this media-controlled world, it's easy to let your thoughts be dominated by what's going on around you. Newspaper and Internet headlines and sound bites describe catastrophes in bold-faced type. Magazine covers display scantily clothed models wearing the latest styles. Your car radio keeps you updated on the latest accidents, crimes, and violence surrounding your community. Television programs portray dysfunctional families living immoral lives. Sometimes we feel overwhelmed by the turmoil or dysfunction around us.

As you prepare for bed with your mind filtering the day's debris, how can you possibly "take every thought captive so that it is obedient to Christ" as the apostle Paul suggests? Keep in mind that Paul traveled through many cities and towns where a licentious lifestyle was the norm. So, he knew the discipline of corralling stray thoughts. It can be as difficult as herding cats.

Philippians 4:8 identifies a way of thinking that you can cultivate before you sleep: "Keep your thoughts on whatever is right or deserves praise: things that are true, honorable, fair, pure, acceptable, or commendable."

When you lie down to sleep tonight, turn your mind to the good things you have in Christ. Note the many times when God has supplied your needs. Think of the power He gives you to be obedient to His directions, then go to sleep.

Praise the God and Father of our Lord Jesus Christ! . . . He comforts us
whenever we suffer. That is why whenever other people suffer, we are able to
comfort them by using the same comfort we have received from God.
2 Corinthians 1:3–4

Heavenly Comforter

It has been said that unless you experience a lack of some kind, you can't know God as Provider. Unless you experience pain and illness, you can't know God as Healer. And unless you experience suffering, you can't know God as Comforter. Through every kind of trouble that you meet along your path, God will reveal another aspect of Himself to you in a very personal way if you're looking.

What are you suffering from? Has grief over a loss overtaken you? Has depression wound its way through your life so as to choke any hope of joy out of it? Has a financial situation dumped an insurmountable load on your shoulders?

Tonight, as you escape from a cold world into the temporary protection of your cozy, warm bed, consider the ways that the Lord has comforted you during periods of suffering. Perhaps He consoled you through the timely encouragement of a friend. Maybe He opened your eyes to see new meaning in a familiar verse of Scripture. Or maybe He painted an otherworldly evening landscape as the sun slipped below a rose-colored horizon—just for you.

A compassionate God bestows comfort on His beloved in tangible ways. He wants you comforted so you can, in turn, comfort someone else. And in so doing, you deepen your relationship with your heavenly Father. What can be more comforting than that?

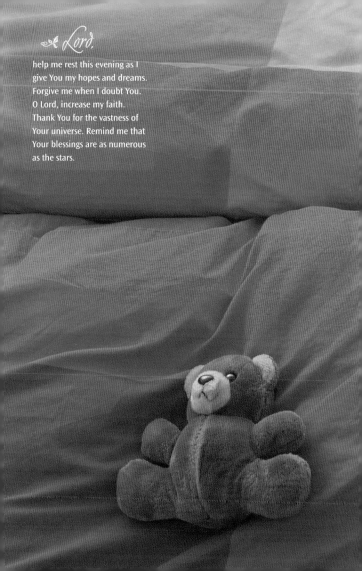

Lord,

help me rest this evening as I
give You my hopes and dreams.
Forgive me when I doubt You.
O Lord, increase my faith.
Thank You for the vastness of
Your universe. Remind me that
Your blessings are as numerous
as the stars.

O Lord,
help me to convey to the
children in my world that
my number-one prayer
for them is that they get
their priorities right from
You. And, as I pray for
them, show me in what
ways I need to adjust my
own priorities so that I
am not too focused on
worldly things.

Keep your mind on things above, not on worldly things.
Colossians 3:2

Priorities

The house rests. The TV is turned off and nightly rituals commence as you head for bed. You pass by sleeping children, taking a quick peek into their rooms. Or you pass images in silver frames of the children in your life who are important to you.

What about the futures of those special children? You may often wonder if they will make good grades, attend college, be popular, excel in sports, or find the right person to marry or the right career to follow. While you cheer along with them any successes they have in life, you also want to somehow show them that those types of successes are never more important than knowing Jesus.

Before you sleep tonight, pray for the children in your world—whether your own, your nieces and nephews, or other children you care about. Ask God to touch their lives and to teach them His ways. Ask that He help them keep their minds on things above, as the apostle Paul advised in his letter to the Colossians. Pray that their attitudes and actions will reflect God and that He will help them stand strong and reject the world's priorities.

And then take a few minutes to think about this for your own life. In what ways are you (or are you not) keeping your mind on things above and not on worldly things? How are your personal priorities shaping up?

Don't love money. Be happy with what you have because
God has said, "I will never abandon you or leave you."
Hebrews 13:5

True Security

You've seen them. Dogs or cats rifling through the trash cans or wandering aimlessly down the street or across your back fence, abandoned by their owners. Animals aren't the only creatures or things that people desert. Many communities have their back streets of abandoned houses, unfinished buildings, and property crammed with broken-down vehicles. Their streets may hold abandoned people, too—the homeless, the helpless, the down-and-outers. The face of abandonment isn't pretty.

Perhaps it's the fear of abandonment that causes people to place money at the top of their "want" list. The story goes that someone asked a rich man, "How much more money do you need to be satisfied?" only to have him reply, "Just a little bit more." Trying to make enough money to be satisfied is an exercise in futility because you'll always want more. Since having money doesn't guarantee contentment, the writer of Hebrews admonishes us to be happy with what we have.

So how can you sleep tonight without worrying about tomorrow? You can be secure in God's presence. You will never be abandoned. When you worship Him with your heart, soul, mind, and strength (Matthew 22:37), you'll find yourself assured and confident of His presence and care. That's much more precious than money.

Dear God,
thank You for Your faithfulness.
Help me to remember that my
happiness doesn't depend on
money, but on knowing and
following You.

Dear Shepherd,

I let go of my tired body
and spirit and submit
myself to Your healing
promise of refreshment.

*I will give those who are weary all they need. I will refresh
everyone who is filled with sorrow.*
Jeremiah 31:25

A Rest That Refreshes

Let's face it. At the end of some days you're completely wiped out. Any combination of negative experiences can make you feel that way. Perhaps your car stalled in the middle of a busy intersection, people squabbled about insignificant issues at your workplace, or you've just learned someone you love has cancer. Your mind and spirit beg to be refreshed. If so, this verse from Jeremiah has a promise you can take to heart: "I will refresh everyone who is filled with sorrow." That promise doesn't have a cancellation clause, or a "good until" date. Just as God promised to restore the Israelites after they were broken in exile, He's always ready to renew and refresh your hope.

In need of renewal? God often works through people and circumstances to accomplish His desires. Reread Jeremiah 31:25, saying the words quietly out loud as a way of owning this promise. Then play one your favorite worship songs. Remember a specific instance of God's goodness. Bask in His love as you pray for Him to bring refreshment in your life—a balm as welcome as a soft hammock on a desert island. Put your day behind you, and absorb the hope that God offers when you lean on Him. Let your hope in Him cover you as you fall asleep.

The one who is testifying to these things says, "Yes, I'm coming soon!" Amen! Come, Lord Jesus! The good will of the Lord Jesus be with all of you. Amen!
Revelation 22:20–21

The Ride of Your Life

If you've ever enjoyed the entertainment of a late summer county fair, you well remember the cotton candy, the carnival games, and the midway—the merry-go-round with its colorful horses, the floating swings, and the sure-to-make-you-sick spinning cars, all culminating in the spectacular Ferris wheel. From the top, you could see the entire fairgrounds, partway around you could yell down to your friends and wave frantically.

But first, you always had to wait in line—sometimes what seemed like an endless line. You counted the times around, you waved to your friends, and you inched forward until you were finally locked in place in your own seat. And then, up you went!

Perhaps you're feeling restless now as you seem to be waiting in an endless line for your heavenly Father to fill you in on what your future holds. You're wondering when He will return and what that will really be like. Take heart. The Lord promises that He will be coming soon, and at just the perfect time.

As you close your eyes tonight, envision your Lord taking you on the ride of your life—for the rest of your time here and on into eternity. Like the Ferris wheel, riding with the Lord will surprise you with a high-flying feeling of excitement. And that ride begins this moment, as you close your eyes and yield to His will and His timing.

Father,

help me to wait on You,
clinging to Your promise
that You will answer
my requests. I wait in
expectation, knowing that
when You return, it will
be the ride of my life!

God,

thank You for being kind and merciful
when I approach Your throne repeatedly.
When I'm tempted to be impatient as I wait
for Your answers, replace my impatience
with enthusiasm for the ride.

We can go confidently to the throne of God's kindness to receive mercy and find kindness, which will help us at the right time.
Hebrews 4:16

The Right Time

You're familiar with the scene—a long trip in a cramped car occupied by you, maybe another adult, and at least one child. The trees and buildings speed by, but even though you're making great time, the inevitable question resonates from the back seat: "Are we there yet?" At first you answer a patient, "No, not yet." You might even smile at the familiarity of the situation. But by the fourth, ninth, and sixteenth times, you're dangerously close to pulling the car over and making everyone else walk.

Been there? So has God. Consider the prayers He often hears. Can you fix this problem now, Lord? Where's the healing I've been asking for? I need an answer about the job today, God. Are You even listening? But His ways are not our ways—thankfully! Like you in the car, He knows that "we aren't there yet." Instead of frustrated threats to end the journey, He provides kindness and mercy when you approach His throne. Because of your high priest, Jesus, you can be assured that God hears your requests (Hebrews 4:14–15). When His answer is "no" or "not yet," He wants you to be confident that He will provide the kindness and mercy you need to be sustained. His boundless grace can move you from "Are we there yet?" to "Let's enjoy the ride together, Lord." Are you willing to trust His timing?

My God will richly fill your every need
in a glorious way through Christ Jesus.
Philippians 4:19

A Want or a Need?

When you were a kid, perhaps a parent taught you the difference between a want and a need. God is also invested in your knowing the difference. He knows what you need and what you want. For example, you may want a zippy, cute little red convertible, but you really just need reliable transportation. You might want some expensive Italian sling-backs, but all you really need is a pair of moderately priced (but still attractive) shoes. You get the picture.

And then there are those below-the-surface needs that you may not even be aware that you have. You may need to be taken out of your comfort zone in order to grow. Maybe you need an abundant measure of forgiveness for a sin you didn't even realize you committed. And you might desperately need a divine touch of joy in a life that has become gray so gradually that you hardly noticed.

Through the divinely inspired words of the apostle Paul, you have the assurance that God knows your needs—even the ones you're not conscious of. And He's so faithful to fill those needs richly—beyond your wildest hopes. When you trust God completely to meet all your needs, He may even take care of a few wants—such as a 75 percent off sale on those sling-backs!

But even if you don't always get what you want, you will always have what you need. And that's infinitely better.

Lord,

You do meet my needs so richly—even ones I'm not aware of. Thank You for doing it gloriously through Jesus, so that each time I see a need and even a want filled, my faith increases even more.

Dear Father,

I give You my load of worries
this evening and trust You to
provide peace for tomorrow
and watch over me as I sleep.

In the morning you'll say, "If only it were evening!" And in the evening you'll say, "If only it were morning!" You'll talk this way because of the things that will terrify you and because of the things you'll see.

Deuteronomy 28:67

The Answer to Fear

With acts of violence peppering the news reports, it's easy to explain why people of the twenty-first century lead fearful lives. Watching the evening news in living color allows the evil in the world to parade through your living room. Why aren't the headlines announcing good news? Fear sells. It also steals away your sense of safety.

A lack of security combined with dissatisfaction with life is enough to make one echo the restless thoughts described in the above passage in Deuteronomy: "It's morning. If only it were evening!" Later, when darkness comes one says, "It's evening. If only it were morning!" What a terrible cycle to be in!

Do you find yourself in a cycle of fear? If so, you need the ultimate fear crusher—the Word of God. Many Bible verses assure you of God's protection in times of danger. For example: "Even when I am afraid, I still trust you. I praise the word of God. I trust God. I am not afraid" (Psalm 56:3–4).

As you are falling to sleep this evening, concentrate on the loving, protective care of God your Father. Meditate on the words of a favorite hymn. Trust God to keep you safe. Bask in His presence. Release your worries to Him and go to sleep.

But I know that my defender lives, and afterwards, he will rise on the earth.
Even after my skin has been stripped off my body, I will see God in my own
flesh. I will see him with my own eyes, not with someone else's.
Job 19:25–27

Put Them in a Box

Some evenings we feel abandoned and helpless in our search for answers to our problems.

You're not the first person to feel abandoned and alone. The words of today's Scripture reading were spoken by Job in the middle of his "bad day" story—the day four messengers told him the terrible news. Different groups of raiders carried off his oxen, donkeys, and camels, then killed his servants. A huge blaze consumed his sheep. Worst news of all: his seven sons and three daughters died after the room they were in collapsed. (See 1:13–22.)

Job sat humiliated and forlorn on an ash heap, his whole body afflicted with sores. He could find neither rest nor sleep. His friends accused him of sinning and his wife suggested that he "curse God and die!" (2:9). But Job handled his difficulties in a manner available to you today: He trusted God to be his defender. Through his suffering, he faithfully believed God would stand with him and give him the hope and strength he needed to survive his plight.

You can follow Job's example. Imagine you are standing in front of an empty box. In your mind place each of your problems in the box. Close the lid, and hand the box to God. Even though your fears might tell you otherwise, trust that God can handle anything inside that box.

God,

I've handed my problems over to You tonight. I'm going to rest in Your presence and trust You to be my defender in every circumstance tomorrow.

Lord,

I don't always admit that I need help. But tonight, I admit that I do. I'm grateful that You willingly take care of me.

When I look at your heavens, the creation of your fingers, the moon
and the stars that you have set in place—what is a mortal that you
remember him or the Son of Man that you take care of him?
Psalm 8:3–4

The Best Caregiver

The Bible describes God's primary nature as all-powerful, all-knowing, present everywhere, and all-loving. No Bible translation, however, uses the word caregiver to describe God.

In today's society, a caregiver is defined as a person whose life is in some way restricted by the responsibility of caring for the needs of a child or dependent adult. In fact, with the aging of the world's population, the need for caregivers has created thriving businesses that provide professional caregivers. Magazines, support groups, newsletters, websites, and books are available to encourage and help parents, spouses, and family members with their care-giving duties.

Although He's never restricted, God is the ultimate Caregiver. David, the psalmist, knew this intimately, having been on the ragged edge of desperation for many years thanks to enemies and family problems. In this passage from Psalm 8, David asks why the Creator of the universe remembers and cares for each human being. The answer is simple: God loves us.

So what kind of care do you need tonight? Are you feeling worn out, stressed out, afraid, or alone? Before you fall asleep, reach out to God in prayer. He's waiting for you to ask for help right now, for He is the best Caregiver of all.

Morning, noon, and night I complain
and groan, and he listens to my voice.
Psalm 55:17

Prayer of the Privileged

You planned for a day as pleasant as a babbling brook. You got a torrential river experience instead. Bad traffic made you late for your first appointment. Another client was a no-show. The kids wouldn't stop arguing. Later on, a good friend called to tell you bad news. Your day definitely merits complaints and groans.

But there is good news. You have a standing invitation to communicate with God. Grab hold of the privilege of prayer. You can pray in any position: standing up, lying down, sitting, kneeling, or even flopped down and sprawled out on the sofa—eyes open or eyes closed. He listens to your voice, whether you whisper in a barely audible voice or just groan in sorrow.

Begin your prayer tonight with a thankful heart toward an amazing God who has the power to handle your life's glitches. Lay your biggest need before Him—the one for which you have no solution. Believe in the impossible—that God can bring something good out of a terrible circumstance.

Now slip into bed, confident that God has heard your voice because you answered His invitation to the privilege of conversation with Him in prayer.

You're Invited

❧ *Heavenly Father,*

thank You for allowing
me to commune with You
through prayer tonight.
I place my faith in Your
power to answer my
prayers.

Lord,

please clear my mind of
the worries and fears that
want to keep me awake
tonight. I praise You for
caring so much about me
that You willingly take on
my worries so that I don't
have to carry them. Give
me a song in the night.

I remember my song in the night and reflect on it. . . . I will
remember the deeds of the LORD. I will remember your ancient miracles.
I will reflect on all your actions and think about what you have done.
Psalm 77:6, 11–12

Song in the Night

Nighttime. A time of precious rest. All too often, however, it can be a time of distress. You lay your head on the pillow only to be assaulted by fear and pain that decides to engage you just as you seek to find quiet. Your mind has been whirling all day, busy with the activities of your life, without room to consider fearful thoughts. But when it's finally dark and quiet . . .

That's when you need a song in the night. That's when you need—to paraphrase the psalm—to reflect on all of God's actions and think about what He has done.

Asaph, writer of this psalm, knew about songs. He was, after all, an important tabernacle musician as well as the author of several psalms. Songs were his passion, his life's work, his calling. Beyond these duties, Asaph also wrote of having a song in the night. Perhaps he was onto something.

What's whirling in your mind tonight? What threatens to keep you tossing and turning? Take a few moments now to petition Jesus to give you a song in the night. Maybe it's a literal praise song you can sing to yourself that will focus your mind on the deeds of the Lord. Maybe it's a passage of Scripture memorized long ago and deeply ingrained in the recesses of your mind.

Then let your song in the night sing you to sleep.

At midnight I wake up to give thanks to you for the regulations, which are based on your righteousness.
Psalm 119:62

Living God's Way

You probably learned at an early age that rules govern your life. In preschool, you needed to put your belongings in your cubbyhole. Grade school introduced a whole new set of rules such as "Put your homework in the red basket." In high school you were issued your driver's license after you passed a test on driving regulations. As an adult, other regulations rule your life: Pay your power bill on time or the electricity gets cut off; pay your taxes on time or you will have to pay a fine; get your kids vaccinated before they start school.

Your walk with God also includes regulations. The writer of Psalm 119 uses many different words for regulations. The most frequently used word is torah, which can mean "teaching" or "instruction" or "law." Other words are principles, commandments, word, and promise. Simply put, God gave you directions that describe how to live a life that is pleasing to Him. In Psalm 119, the psalmist thanks God for His regulations.

Do you approach God's rules with the same thankfulness? God always appreciates it when you thank Him for His guidance in your life. Before you sleep this evening, why not tell God how grateful you are for His clear, biblical instructions. Sleep in peace, for God loves a grateful heart.

Lord,
thank You for Your
Word tonight. Help me
remember its directions
tomorrow so that my life
may be pleasing to You.

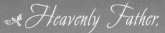
Heavenly Father,

Thank You for loving me
and being with me along
life's journey. I know I can
rest tonight because You
care for me.

> *The LORD is near to everyone who prays to him, to every faithful person who prays to him. He fills the needs of those who fear him. He hears their cries for help and saves them.*
>
> Psalm 145:18–19

A Cry for Help

Nothing tugs at the heart quite like the sound of a crying child. Your brain kicks into action with a set of questions: Is the child hungry? Tired? Hurt? Afraid? If it's your child, you go as quickly as you can to check out his/her needs. If it's not your child, you look around for the child's caregiver. You become concerned if the crying doesn't cease, if you sense the child's needs aren't being met. You can't really relax until the sound stops.

When you decided to follow Jesus, you became a child of God. Does that mean you will never again experience troubles or sorrow or pain? No. It means you have full access to God, the true source of life. God hears every cry uttered by His children loud and clear. This is David's message in Psalm 145. It was one David fully believed in. The book of Psalms is filled with David's cries for help.

Before you sleep tonight, praise God for three situations in which you felt His intervention and power. Praise Him for His presence. Freely share your current needs with Him. For just as a mother seeks to still her child's cry, God stands ready to give you the peace and rest your heart desires.

*Do not brag about tomorrow, because you do not know
what another day may bring.*
Proverbs 27:1

To Plan or Not to Plan?

Ever make plans that were thwarted by an outcome you didn't predict? We all have times when we think we know what tomorrow might bring. This verse in Proverbs is played out in a parable Jesus tells in the Gospel of Luke. In that story, a rich man made plans to build larger barns in which to store his abundant crops. His plans for the future, however, were in vain, as God announced that the man would die that night.

Does this mean that making plans for your future is wrong? No. Go ahead and prepare a budget, work schedule, or a move to another place. But be sure to allow for God's guidance as you plan. Jeremiah 29:11 explains why this is so important: "I know the plans that I have for you, declares the LORD. They are plans for peace and not disaster, plans to give you a future filled with hope."

As you get ready for bed tonight, do you have doubts about your future plans? It's not the time to be self-reliant. Pray for wisdom and direction from God regarding the course your life should take. He may guide you down an unexpected path—a path you might never have anticipated or chosen on your own. And because you don't know what tomorrow may bring, how wonderful to go to sleep tonight entrusting tomorrow to the One who does know.

Thank You,

God, for loving me so much that You have a special plan for my life. Help me to submit my plans to You and to follow Your Spirit's leading during my journey into the future.

Father,

this time of rest is so important. It helps me see know how generous You have been. My life is blessed with so many riches. Thank
You for Your great gifts. Help me to use them wisely and never
forget to praise You.

Therefore, a time of rest and worship exists for God's people.
Hebrews 4:9

Such Treasures to Behold!

Have you ever had a time when one crisis after another seemed to occur? Everyone has such times periodically. Maybe that's why God made the commandment to set a whole day aside for rest, as this verse in Hebrews mentions.

If it's true we all have trials, it is also true that we all have treasures! Slowing down helps us see the great riches we have received. No matter what problems you are dealing with now, when you reflect on all God's gifts, you'll feel refreshed and renewed.

Our gifts from God are magnificent. The gift of our amazingly complex bodies can inspire us. The gift of family can comfort us. The gift of creation, in all its regal forms, calls out for attention. The gifts of a warm house, inspiring words to read, a soft quilt, an aromatic cup of tea—these are blessings we can feel, smell, and appreciate.

Imagine how a treasure hunter rejoices over the discovery of jewels. Just think—your God-given treasure box is always available. At this time of night, you can remember the commandment to rest. With your treasure box of blessings from God open to appreciate, you can relax easily. Settle into bed like a queen. What a wonder it is to have been lavished with so many blessings.

Open your treasure box now. Dig deeply into this bounty of heavenly gifts.

*Look at the sky and see. Who created these things? Who
brings out the stars one by one? He calls them all by name.*
Isaiah 40:26

A Brilliant Message

It's the work of an artist—carefully crafted, piece by piece, down
to every detail. What was He thinking, this artist-God, as He
painted the sky with these billions of clusters of gaseous light? Imagine Him smiling as He looked at all that He had created. Knowing the
lifespan of each ball of fire, He also knew the wonder and amazement
that we, His children, would feel as we look up. It's too big for us to
imagine, but not for Him. Even the millions and billions of stars are
not overwhelming to our Father. He knows them by name. He knows
their size, their exact location, their history, and not only that: He created them all. And He created you.

Whenever you doubt if God knows what frustrations you face,
look at the sky and see. Look up. If you're unsure if God truly has your
best interests in mind, look up. When life gets overwhelming and it
feels like you're all alone, stop, and look up.

Every night, your Father is sending you a brilliant message of His
love for you. He's shouting His greatness and care for you. In the
evening, even in the darkness of night, you are not alone. You have a
Father who loves you, and is powerful enough to provide for you. He
knows your name, and wishes you a good night's rest.

Father,

I look at the stars and remember Your greatness. I look at the stars and remember Your love. As I look up tonight, I will remember that You are good.

Father,

I'm surrounded by daily
chaos and sometimes find it
hard to believe that I can feel
peaceful, but I know You can
and will provide for my needs.
Help me to trust You, to know
Your peace, and to sleep
soundly tonight.

*I'm leaving you peace. I'm giving you my peace.
I don't give you the kind of peace that the
world gives. So don't be troubled or cowardly.*
John 14:27

Peace beyond Understanding

All around us, we're bombarded with cries for peace or peaceful solutions to problems. We see peace symbols on jewelry or scrawled across signs, but peace never really comes.

That's why Jesus promised His peace, which is not of this world. Although He would soon be killed, His death would bring about the ultimate peace—a reconciliation between God and man. The prophet Isaiah saw it centuries before: "He was wounded for our rebellious acts. He was crushed for our sins. He was punished so that we could have peace, and we received healing from his wounds" (Isaiah 53:5).

Jesus' peace does not mean absence of conflict. His peace does not mean quiet solace for the rest of our lives. It's a different kind of peace, not the peace the world might attempt to give, or peace as the world would define it. Instead, it's a deep inner core of peace in the midst of conflict, in the center of difficulty, in the eye of the storm. This peace grounds you, holds you, protects you, helps you keep it together on the inside no matter what's going on outside.

Are you in need of peace? Meditate on Jesus' promise of peace. He said to His disciples, and to you, "I've told you this so that my peace will be with you. In the world you'll have trouble. But cheer up! I have overcome the world" (John 16:33).

I will look to the LORD. I will wait for God to save me.
I will wait for my God to listen to me.
Micah 7:7

Resolved to Wait

Waiting is hard. As children, we all struggled with waiting: We wanted Christmas to come tomorrow, wanted dessert before dinner, and wanted our turn on the swing to be right now, rather than once our brother or sister was done.

Now, even though we're "all grown-up," waiting isn't easier. Sometimes we're waiting for things that are urgent—the tax refund or that next paycheck to arrive, a phone call about that new job or commission, or a loved one to come home safely. When Micah speaks of waiting in these verses, he's not talking about waiting for ice cream or a turn on the monkey bars. He, too, is waiting for something truly important. He's waiting for his people to be freed from oppression, to be given their lives and country back.

Is it easy to wait? Absolutely not, but Micah resolves in his heart that he "will wait" because he knows that the only real answer to his worries comes from above. This is an example of waiting with anticipation. He knows that something good is about to happen. It's like the waiting for the fireworks to start on the Fourth of July. You have no doubt that you'll see them across the sky.

What are you waiting for? Will you trust God to answer in His time? Can you say with confidence that His timing is perfect, even when it seems otherwise from your perspective? Pray that He will give you that confidence tonight.

Father,

I'm impatient. There are questions I'd like answered and problems I'd like solved, and if I were in control, I'd fix them now. But I'm not in control—You are. Help me to trust You. Even though it's not easy, I will wait.

Lord,

instill in me an undeniable
desire to follow You and
Your commands. Teach me
to see the joy in obeying
You, even in the face of
oppression.

*My eyes are wide-open throughout the
nighttime hours to reflect on your word.*
Psalm 119:148

Deposits in God's Bank

For some, a sleepless night is the ultimate enemy to wrestle against and hopefully win. But for the writer of Psalm 119, a sleepless night was filled with the potential for connecting with God. In Psalm 119:145–146, he pleaded with the Lord to save him. "I have called out with all my heart. Answer me, O LORD. I want to obey your laws. I have called out. Save me, so that I can obey your written instructions." A few verses later, he explained how he spent the time reflecting on God's Word. Believing that the Lord would guide him, he praised the Lord for His goodness and vowed to obey His laws.

Note that he didn't spend the time grumbling about wakefulness. After all, wakefulness seemed to be a conscious choice in order to commune with God. Instead, he took his worry and deposited it in his heavenly Father's bank, then "withdrew" the truths of God's Word.

What keeps you awake at night? Worries? Pain? Anticipation for what tomorrow might bring? Tonight, ask God to help you dwell on His promises. He promises to love you, guide you, and answer you. Why not make a withdrawal from God's bank of wisdom and promises? Enter that place of wonder. Discover the exhilaration of following Christ!

Special Excerpt from the Companion Devotional

120 Devotions to Start Your Day

quiet*reflections* of hope

Revell
a division of Baker Publishing Group
www.RevellBooks.com

Available wherever books are sold

*Don't you know that you are God's temple
and that God's Spirit lives in you?
1 Corinthians 3:16*

God's Temple

Solomon built one. Zerubbabel built one. You are one—a living temple fashioned and crafted by God Himself. Ancient temples used gold, silver, and precious metals as symbols of purity and holiness; they were places people believed their gods lived. Solomon's magnificent temple (read about it in 1 Kings 6) and Zerubbabel's temple (a rebuilding of Solomon's temple after its destruction by the Babylonians—see 2 Kings 25 and Ezra 3) were places for God's presence among His people. However, with Christ came a new living temple made of people who believe in Him and who are made beautiful by the presence of the Holy Spirit within each one.

Maybe this morning you don't feel like a beautiful temple of God. The past casts shadows around every nook and cranny—whether from bad choices, poor decisions, or costly mistakes. Seasons of neglect or strife have caused crumbling walls or a cracking foundation.

No matter what you have built in your life before, today is a new day! A day to be renewed and encouraged, knowing that the Holy Spirit is there with you, beside you, in you. He is ready and waiting to be your source of strength and hope this day, especially in the middle of your challenges. Choose today to be a living temple founded on Christ and transformed by the Holy Spirit—a place of character where God resides, a place of beauty where God is reflected, a place of sanctuary where God is welcomed.

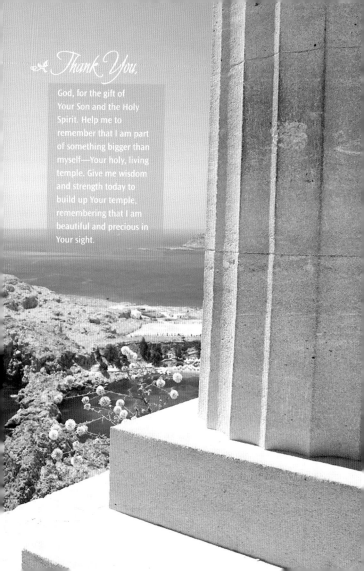

Thank You,

God, for the gift of Your Son and the Holy Spirit. Help me to remember that I am part of something bigger than myself—Your holy, living temple. Give me wisdom and strength today to build up Your temple, remembering that I am beautiful and precious in Your sight.

Let my teachings come down like raindrops. Let my words drip like dew, like gentle rain on grass, like showers on green plants.
Deuteronomy 32:2

Soul Refreshment

How refreshing is the Word of the Lord! The Father wants His Word to be soothing and nourishing. He wants His teachings to "come down like raindrops"—refreshing, cleansing, satisfying, just like your morning shower.

But sometimes it doesn't seem that way. You may at times feel that your devotions seem stale, your prayer time feels perfunctory, you're not feeling refreshed by God's Word at all. What can you do to enliven this time with God so that you come away feeling freshly showered? Perhaps it's a question of immersion. You don't get fully clean by sticking just your toe in the shower. You won't get the full effect of God's Word until you're immersed in it, until the teachings come down like raindrops around you.

God's Word is often compared to water, that most valuable and wholesome resource. Remember the blessed man that the psalmist praises in Psalm 1. The study of God's law, the Word of the Lord, makes this man "like a tree planted beside streams—a tree that produces fruit in season and whose leaves do not wither" (Psalm 1:3). The psalmist knows that a diligent study of the Word of God helps him produce fruit and keeps him from withering.

Remember that the Father wants His teachings to refresh you. Let today be one of the days when His Word is as soothing as "showers on green plants."

Father,

let Your teaching be as
refreshing as soft rain
showers. Thank You for
blessing me with Your
Word, which will continue
to strengthen me through
both good days and bad.